The Open University

Arts: A Fourth Level Course

Units 29–31

Thought and Reality: Central Themes in Wittgenstein's Philosophy

CERTAINTY
A discussion of
Wittgenstein's notes *On Certainty*

Prepared by Carolyn Wilde
for the Course Team

The Open University Press

Front cover:

This tree stands in New Court, Trinity College, Cambridge, the college of Moore and Wittgenstein

The Open University Press
Walton Hall, Milton Keynes
MK7 6AA

First published 1976. Reprinted with corrections 1977

Copyright © 1977 The Open University

Designed by the Media Development Group of the Open University.

Produced in Great Britain by
Technical Filmsetters Europe Limited, 76 Great Bridgewater Street, Manchester M1 5JY

ISBN 0 335 05213 4

This text forms part of an Open University course. The complete list of units in the course appears at the end of this text.

For general availability of supporting material referred to in this text, please write to Open University Educational Enterprises Limited, 12 Cofferidge Close, Stony Stratford, Milton Keynes MK11 1BY, Great Britain.

Further information on Open University courses may be obtained from the Admissions Office, The Open University, P.O. Box 48, Walton Hall, Milton Keynes, MK7 6AB.

2.1

CONTENTS

ABBREVIATIONS

Abbreviations of titles of works of Wittgenstein, as used in text:

T   *Tractatus Logico-Philosophicus*
BB   *The Blue and Brown Books*
PI   *Philosophical Investigations*
Z   *Zettel*
OC *On Certainty*

INTRODUCTION

The topic and its treatment

Wittgenstein was working in a tradition of philosophy which is often said to have begun with Descartes and with the assumption that the theory of knowledge is the fundamental topic of philosophy. In the first four units of this course you studied the roots of what have been a central pair of assumptions in this tradition: namely, that knowledge forms a system with specifiable foundations, and that the task of a philosophical theory of knowledge is, first, to establish those truths which—in virtue of being certain and indubitable—form those foundations and, second, to show how all other genuine claims to knowledge are logically related to these truths. Without the possibility of appeal, at some ultimate point, to these foundations, there would seem to be no objective way of settling any issue which would be both rational and decisive: no way, in other words, of justifying even our most commonly held beliefs. Notoriously, there have been many suggestions that certainty of the required kind is unobtainable and, hence, that genuine knowledge is impossible. But if the suggestions are on the right lines, then there must be something wrong with this model of knowledge. For aren't there a multitude of things we do know for certain? Wouldn't it just be philosophical pedantry to deny this?

In the first half of this century, the philosopher G. E. Moore, in some now-famous lectures and articles, and in conversations with students and philosophers in Cambridge, addressed himself specifically to this issue of whether anything can be known, with certainty, to be true. Wittgenstein was particularly struck by some of the things Moore said, and during the last eighteen months of his life he gave them a lot of thought. The notes he made during this period have been put together and published under the title *On Certainty*. Moore had given several examples of things he claimed to *know*, with certainty, to be true: such things as 'Here is one hand' (said whilst holding up his hand), '*That* is a tree' (said whilst pointing to a tree), and 'I have never been far from the surface of the earth'. Wittgenstein thought that there was something very misleading in Moore's attempt to counter sceptical arguments by asserting that he did know the things about which sceptical doubts had been raised. But he did not deny nor doubt the truth of any of the things Moore claimed to know. In fact, he thought that there was something very significant in Moore's choice of examples.

Our job in these units will be both to try to establish why Wittgenstein thought it misleading of Moore to claim to know these sorts of things, and to find out what he nevertheless thought significant about Moore's examples, in relation to the problems posed by the traditional sceptical arguments. Asking these questions, though, will not entangle us merely in some local issue between Moore and Wittgenstein. It involves challenging that model of knowledge which has had such a central place in philosophy since Descartes and in the light of which the application of sceptical questions has had such disastrous—or paradoxical—results. In particular, it involves questioning the standards, which seem to be required on philosophical reflection, of grounds for making any statement or claim to knowledge. This issue lies at the heart of the subject-matter of A402, the theme of the relations between language, thought and reality. For an initial question of philosophy might seem to be: 'How, from our ideas (some of which are of things imagined or dreamt), from our perceptions, feelings and fallible judgements, can we know how things really are?' And such a question may implicitly involve thinking of

5

knowledge as consisting of some sort of a relation between what is thought and a reality independent of that thought, with which the thought corresponds. In the early units of this course you studied some of the complexities involved in such a model. In these units we turn again to these matters—this time, however, not in preparation for examining Wittgenstein's ideas in the *Tractatus*, which was an extremely sophisticated working-out of the logical requirements of such a model, but in order to see how the ideas he developed in later works bear on these questions.

I should perhaps warn you that I put forward a sympathetic reading of *On Certainty* in these units. I try to fill out some of the ideas which I believe to be explicitly or implicitly contained in the text, and in order to do so I have drawn upon views about sense and meaning which I have taken from my reading of Wittgenstein's previous writings—particularly the *Philosophical Investigations*. To the extent that I have done this successfully and clearly, these units should enable you to revise and think further about some of the central ideas you've already been working with in A402. However, although *On Certainty*, unlike the previous texts which you've been studying, is a close and concentrated treatment of just one topic, it is nonetheless a collection of notes which Wittgenstein made for his own use, and not a systematic presentation of developed ideas. So any attempt to elucidate the ideas of *On Certainty* will be, even more than usual with Wittgenstein, controversial and likely to be inadequate. Please read these units in conjunction with your own close reading of *On Certainty*: it's not a very long work, and in one sense can be read through quite quickly. I shall at several points refer to or ask you to read particular sections, but do read the whole work through at least once before the end of the three-week period, at a pace which gives you a general conception, independently of the way I present them, of Wittgenstein's ideas.

Prescribed reading

There is very little other reading needed to work through these units, besides *On Certainty*. For working through section 1 you will need:

> Hume, *An Enquiry Concerning Human Understanding*, Bobbs-Merrill edition

and for Section 3:

> A. J. Ayer, 'Wittgenstein on Certainty', in G. Vesey (ed.) *Understanding Wittgenstein*, Macmillan.

At the end of the units you will find a list of some other books and articles you may find it interesting to read.

Acknowledgements

In writing these units I have been very grateful for the help of Stuart Brown, Susan Khin Zaw, Oswald Hanfling and Godfrey Vesey of the A402 Course Team, and of Ephraim Borowski of Hertford College, Oxford and David Pole of King's College London, all of whom took on the task of trying to sort out the units' philosophical unclarity, especially that springing from my inadequate use of English. I am especially grateful to Jim Hopkins of King's College London for his pains in trying to extract some clear statements of the arguments used.

I have made free use of material by, and ideas remembered from conversations with, Professor P. Winch of King's College, London, of an article very kindly lent to me by Miles Burnyeat of University College London on 'Examples in Epistemology: Socrates, Theaetetus and G. E. Moore' and of early drafts of Ilham Dilman's book *Induction and Deduction* which Dr. Dilman generously sent to me some years ago.

1 PHILOSOPHICAL SCEPTICISM

1.1 THE QUESTION OF MOORE'S ANTAGONISTS

When Moore stood up and said that it was certain that he was, as his audience could see, standing speaking in a room, and not lying down in the open air either whispering or singing, who did he think needed convincing?[1]

In this section I want, not so much to identify 'the sceptic'—since there have in fact been few philosophers who held to the position of scepticism—as to make some general points about the different sorts of considerations entering into sceptical arguments and their roles in various more positive philosophical positions. You should find that much of what I say is familiar from your studies in the first six units of A402.

On the same occasion Moore speaks of 'many philosophers' who use certain arguments to allege that 'nobody ever has known for certain anything about a world external to his mind', and he goes on to discuss one of these arguments in particular, namely the argument from dreaming. On another occasion, when discussing scepticism, he specifically mentions Russell, who certainly did seem to take this argument seriously. On page 10 of *The Problems of Philosophy*,[2] for instance, Russell says that 'there is no logical impossibility in the supposition that the whole of life is a dream in which we ourselves create all the objects that come before us'. Russell goes on to admit that there is no reason whatever to suppose that this is true. Nevertheless, it remains the case that 'because we cannot rule the hypothesis of dreaming out as impossible, it must be admitted that we can never *prove* the existence of things other than ourselves and our experiences'.

Descartes' first principle of philosophy was that 'in order to examine into the truth, it is necessary once in one's life to doubt of all things, so far as this is possible' (*The Principles of Philosophy*, Principle 1),[3] and in order to *make* it possible to doubt such things as that he was sitting in his study, he likewise appealed to the argument from dreaming. In the first radio programme for this course, Stuart Brown spoke about Descartes' use of the facts of dreaming and sense-deception to undermine the belief that there are certain sorts of things existing in the world independently of our ideas of them. He ended the programme by saying that the question whether or not it makes sense to say that the whole of life is a dream, or that we are in a constant state of sense-delusion, has remained a subject of philosophical controversy ever since. Moore can be seen, then, as addressing himself to those philosophers, including among others Descartes and Russell, who held that nothing can really be certain unless it is provable or logically impossible to doubt.

You may still feel some impatience with such a supposition as that, for all we know (or for all *I* know, as it would have to be), the whole of life is a dream; or you may think that this is not a real enough supposition for serious attention. The point, however, is that the philosopher who raises such questions is not necessarily just indulging in clever sophistical argument, but may be enquiring into our very standards of rationality and knowledge. Descartes, in the *Meditations*, was impressed by the fact that he could find no conclusive signs by means of which he could distinguish clearly between ideas

[1] He began his Howison lecture, 'Certainty', at the University of California in 1941, in this way. The lecture is published in *Philosophical Papers*, Allen and Unwin, 1959.
[2] Oxford, 1959 ed.
[3] *The Philosophical Works of Descartes*, Cambridge, page 218 (Everyman ed., page 165).

which he had previously thought of as ideas of the world, and ideas which are *just* ideas, such as he experienced in dreams or illusions. Consequently, he asked, how *can* we distinguish those ideas which are trustworthy grounds for knowledge from those which are not? He thought it necessary to apply the systematic programme of doubt to all possible beliefs, as a means of answering this question. But his wish was to use such scepticism only as a means of finally validating a certain method of enquiry and corpus of knowledge; he saw his position, not as the negative one of promoting scepticism, but as, ultimately, the positive one of overcoming it.

For all this, however, by his sceptical arguments Descartes in fact gave life to the idea that there is a gap between, on the one hand, our thoughts and beliefs and, on the other, the things we think about. And the arguments he used to establish such a gap have had far more influence in subsequent philosophy than his attempts to bridge it.

In *On Certainty*, when Wittgenstein alludes to the target of Moore's remarks, he speaks, not of the sceptic, but of the 'idealist' (e.g. at *OC* 19, 24, 37). The idealist claims, not so much that 'nobody has ever known for certain anything about a world external to his mind', to use Moore's phrase, as that the proper objects of knowledge are, in one of many senses, 'dependent' on the mind. Thus although Wittgenstein indicates that Moore is addressing himself to those who claim to *doubt* 'the existence of the external world' (as at *OC* 20), the focus of his own interest is the tension between the realist and the idealist (see *OC* 37 and 59). At *OC* 37, however, he uses the phrase 'the scepticism of the idealist'. So what we need to do, in the first instance, is to indicate some of the interconnections between scepticism, idealism and realism. I intend to do this by using as a base some of the things David Hume considers in the *Enquiry Concerning Human Understanding*.

1.2 SOME SCEPTICAL CONSIDERATIONS IN HUME'S *ENQUIRY*

1.2.1 *Enquiry*, Section 12, Part 1

Hume is usually acknowledged as a major influence on the emphasis on scepticism in the tradition in which Wittgenstein was writing. He had, however, a very complex and ambivalent attitude towards the sceptical arguments. For our purposes we shall confine our attention to two brief sections from the *Enquiry*.[1] Please now read Part 1 of Section 12, and list the different arguments which Hume says can be used by the sceptic against the evidence of the senses concerning the nature and independent existence of the world. Note also any points of contact or contrast with sceptical arguments which you have studied in earlier units in relation to other philosophers, such as Descartes, Russell or Berkeley.

Before we attend to the arguments Hume discusses, it is worth noting a small point which takes the question of the seriousness, or relevance, of philosophical scepticism a little further. Hume introduces the section with some remarks apparently connecting religious belief and atheism with beliefs and disbeliefs about dragons and giants. There are many beliefs which can have a central and important place in people's lives and projects—beliefs, however, about which there is either much dispute or which non-believers consider to be clearly wrong. At one time the belief that the earth was at the centre of the universe played an unquestioned role in a whole system of

[1] *Enquiry Concerning Human Understanding*, Bobbs-Merrill edition.

beliefs and activities. The sceptic's questions can be seen as a challenge to show that we are justified in being sure, now, of *our* most fundamental beliefs. The problem can seem to be that, unless our forms of thought can be justified in terms of some objective standards, we apparently have no means of distinguishing knowledge from variable opinion, science or medicine from superstition, or, in another sphere, morality from convention. In the last part of the units, I shall indicate how Wittgenstein's treatment of the topic of certainty does not meet this challenge but is an attempt to undercut it.

Hume distinguishes three arguments, or considerations, which can lead to scepticism:

(a) 'Those which are derived from the imperfection or fallaciousness of our organs' (in the sixth paragraph). This I shall call *the argument from error*.

(b) 'Those which teach us that nothing can ever be present to the mind but an image or perception' (beginning at paragraph eight). This I shall call *the argument from unknown causes*.

(c) *The argument from primary and secondary qualities*, in the penultimate paragraph.

You may have listed what Hume describes as 'antecedent scepticism', in the third paragraph, as a separate argument. I haven't done so because Hume doesn't actually discuss any particular sceptical argument, but simply asserts his opposition to the general Cartesian strategy for applying sceptical arguments. We cannot *start*, he claims, by being critical of our faculties of perception and attempting to *prove* their trustworthiness by reason alone. Whether Hume is right in this matter remains to be seen. His statement of opposition to the strategy of Cartesian doubt is a statement of his general empiricist position in the dispute about what should be acknowledged as the basic starting-points in any account of knowledge: the principles of reason or the items of experience. This fundamental difference between himself and Descartes, however, does have a bearing, as we shall see, on the fact that Hume sees the considerations entering into the argument from error as 'but trite topics'.

(a) The argument from error

This is the sort of argument which exploits the facts of delusion and illusion. An oar or a stick, half-immersed in water, appears to be bent. In some circumstances we see two things where there is in fact only one. Descartes' example, in *Meditation VI*,[1] is the fact that a square tower can appear from a distance to be round. Such discrepancies are easily corrected, Hume says, by taking the medium, or the distance, or whatever special conditions are relevant, into account. Descartes, however, did not think that facts of this sort could be so easily dismissed. He cited the examples in order to ask: how can we be sure in *any* given case that a judgement based upon evidence of the senses is not mistaken, if we discover that these same senses sometimes lead us to be mistaken? A more contemporary reply to Descartes has been to say that, if we are to be able to talk of non-veridical perception at all, then some perceptions must be veridical. But this, in itself, is not an adequate reply since, if our confidence is not going to be undermined in the way Descartes suggests, we need a way of knowing *which* perceptions are veridical. Descartes might press his case by emphasizing that the resolution of any doubt in these sorts of cases rests ultimately on other evidence from the senses.

---

[1] Cambridge ed., page 189 (Everyman ed., page 131).

9

The difference between Hume and Descartes here leads back to the question of that more radical approach which Hume has already dismissed. Descartes supposes that these facts of error in judgement require us to find some general proof, some 'reasoning deduced from some original principle which cannot possibly be fallacious or deceitful' (as Hume describes Descartes' programme), regarding the trustworthiness of the senses. That is, he calls for some reason for trusting our senses *at all*. Hume, by contrast, says that accuracy in judgement will be a matter of applying the criteria appropriate to each case. He concedes that reason certainly does come into play, but it is clear that he is talking about reasoning concerning the facts of particular cases.

(b) The argument from unknown causes

The arguments which Hume takes more seriously depend not so much on the possibility of error, as on the impossibility of giving any account of what the proper objects of knowledge are. In the case of the previous argument, I referred to Descartes' insistence on the inadequacy of any evidence from particular experiences and to his suggestion that, for all we know, our senses may always be deceiving us. By emphasizing these points, Descartes has already moved from noting that we may be mistaken as to what is in fact the case *about some object* to the suggestion that maybe there are *no such things at all* as the objects which we think we see. Hume approaches this argument from a different direction. We acquire knowledge of the world through perception of it. Yet certain considerations can lead us to suppose that what we *directly* perceive is not some situation existing independently of our perception of it, but an idea, or image as Hume calls it here, which mediates between us and the object. As we perceive any object its size and shape appear to differ according to our position or distance from it; yet the object itself does not change in virtue of these factors. There are also, to use the example from the previous argument again, situations in which we see double. But the example here has a different point. It is used, not to ask which image is the correct one or how can we establish how many objects there actually are, but to say that *neither* of the two things we see when we see double, nor *any* of the perceptual ideas, are the real object. This is the familiar distinction between *ideas* and *things*. It is a distinction which seems to become necessary when we try to account for the fact that the objects we speak of remain the same, whereas our perceptions of them vary. This view of perception, then, which Hume describes as very reasonable, apparently exposes a gap between our perceptions and the world such that it becomes problematical how these perceptions provide us with knowledge of the world at all.

Hume puts forward three arguments, in the eleventh and twelfth paragraphs of Part 1, against the possibility of proving that 'the perceptions of the mind can be caused by external objects' which they resemble. These arguments are again interesting in connection with Descartes. In *Meditation III* Descartes also puts forward arguments why he should be sceptical concerning his inclination to believe that his ideas 'proceed from certain objects which are outside of me' and to which the ideas are similar. Both Hume and Descartes refer again to the facts of dreaming and hallucinating. Such facts show us that we can have ideas which to all intents and purposes appear to be ideas of things actually existing and of situations actually happening, but which do not, in actuality, 'arise from anything external'. But there is a difference in the way Hume and Descartes each respond to the question how we can know whether or not the ideas resemble the objects. According to Hume, all our ideas must surely arise from sense experience and so, obviously, we can have no knowledge of the connection of objects to perceptions.

✳ see argument 'c'.

When he says that 'the supposition of such a connection is...without any foundation in reasoning', he means that the reasons he has given (which include this empiricist assumption about the origins of all our ideas) show that the supposition has no foundation. Reason, however, plays a different role in Descartes' account. Descartes argues that he can have two completely diverse ideas of an object. By this he does not mean two perceptions of an object, such as the two perceptions of the table Hume spoke of, which present the table as having two different sizes. Descartes instances having two ideas of the sun: one of these ideas, he says, derives its origin from the senses, and according to it the sun seems to be exceedingly small; but his other idea is 'derived from astronomical reasonings', and in accordance with this idea the sun appears to be several times greater than the earth. The two ideas cannot both resemble the same sun; and *reason*, Descartes says, makes him believe that the idea which he gained by looking at the sun is the one which is more dissimilar to it.

How do you think Descartes is using the term 'reason'?

This fact about the size of the sun is deduced from other facts, or theories established in science. But, of course, for Descartes, the chain of deductive reasoning which is used to establish such facts can be traced back via the ultimate principles of reasoning to the indubitable truths upon which all knowledge is founded. And this involves a quite fundamental difference between Hume and Descartes about the problem (they both *agree* there is a problem) of ensuring that our ideas are caused by external objects and not put into our minds either 'by the energy of the mind itself' or by some deceiving demon (which Hume refers to as an 'unknown spirit'). Hume, in this part of the *Enquiry*, accepts that we are left with the problem: we cannot *justify* our belief that there is any object which 'preserves its existence uniform and entire, independent of the situation of intelligent beings, who perceive or contemplate it'. (At the end of Part II of Section 12, however, he says clearly that, although the sceptical conclusions cannot be refuted, they pale against those 'powerful principles of our nature' in accordance with which we live and act. This will be significant when we read Wittgenstein's more positive position in section 4 of these units.) Descartes, however, is laying down the basis for his whole position by taking on this demand for a justification. He hopes to show by *reason* that we are justified in trusting the evidence of our senses and believing that there is a world of corporeal substances existing independently of our ideas. His appeal to God, whose nature and existence he attempts to establish by reason, is an appeal to something which *transcends*, or goes beyond, experience: to something which bridges the gap between ideas and things. Hume's dismissal of Descartes' move here is a bit hasty. The veracity of the Supreme Being is not, on Descartes' account, all that we are concerned with in this matter, as Hume says it is. The bridge which Descartes establishes is thus not so 'unexpected', in view of Descartes' approach to the place of reason in knowledge. This difference between Hume and Descartes is, of course, directly connected with the contrast between views described as 'idealist' and 'realist', a point which we will take up in section 1.4.

(c)   The argument from primary and secondary qualities

This argument turns on the distinction made by Locke, Descartes and the natural scientists of their day, such as Boyle and Galileo, between, on the one hand, the ideas we have of an object in virtue of its effect on us or its interaction with our faculties, and, on the other hand, the qualities it has which cause or are the source of the effects. This argument, then, is also based on a distinction between ideas and things. Both Berkeley and Hume took it to be the same sort of distinction between ideas and things as the one at the centre of the previous argument. But I think they were mistaken in doing so. I think there is room for looking at Locke's distinction between primary and secondary qualities as an attempt to give a fuller account of a distinction which Locke already accepts: that is, the distinction between the world as it is described in terms of our experience of it and the world as the object of scientific enquiry.

In the passage of the *Enquiry* which we are considering, Hume uses Berkeley's arguments to question the distinction between primary and secondary qualities: according to the distinction, the so-called secondary qualities of an object, such as its heat or colour, are ideas or perceptions which differ according to the position and condition of the observer. But similarly, Hume argues, an object's extension— its size or shape—, which we perceive, also differs according to the angle or point of perception. If, however, we take away all the *particular* perception-relative ideas of an object, then we are left with no idea of it at all.

Now although this argument has the same conclusion as the previous one, namely that we can have no knowledge of objects which are supposed to exist independently of, and be the cause of, particular ideas or experiences, it is directed against a particular view as to the nature of such objects. This view is the corpuscular theory of matter, put forward by Boyle and Galileo and championed by Locke. When Hume says that his third sceptical topic is 'derived from the most profound philosophy', he is referring to this view of matter and the physical world, advanced in what we would now describe as the natural sciences.

Hume's and Berkeley's criticism of Locke's distinction between primary and secondary qualities is cogent only given the assumption, basic to their epistemology, that all knowledge must be compounded from the immediate data of sensory experience, and given the additional claim that the data of any judgement are ideas and not the things of which they are ideas. Granted these conditions, the notion of the physical world put forward as the proper object of scientific enquiry is unfounded. In Units 3–4, section 4, however, you were given some indication how *Locke's* allegiance to this claim about the data of judgement might be questioned. Knowledge of things in so far as they affect our bodies is to be distinguished from knowledge of their essential nature. In this respect, Locke shares something of Descartes' emphasis on the use of reason in establishing truths about the nature of the world. That is, he shares the view that there is a distinction between mere perceptual, and scientific, knowledge of the real world.

You may remember Locke's example, cited during his discussion of the distinction between primary and secondary qualities, of what happens when you pound an almond (*Essay*, II. viii. 20).[1] By pounding the almond, which is doing something which physically changes its shape and texture, I *thereby* change its colour and taste. So the latter, which are examples of secondary qualities, must be dependent, in some way, on the former. If understood in this way, Locke's argument by experiment here establishes a difference between different kinds of qualities, which Hume's and Berkeley's argument does not account for. Nevertheless, it does not, of itself, establish that things have an essential constitution, the elements of which are not, in Hume's sense, 'mind-dependent'. The argument, then, that there can be no distinction between primary and secondary qualities, shows, according to

[1] Fontana ed., page 116.

Hume, that 'the opinion of external existence' is ill-founded. But this claim does depend, as he says at the end of Part 1, on the validity of 'the principle of reason that all sensible qualities are in the mind, not in the object'. So Hume's third argument is to a large extent dependent on his second.

✳ See Argument 'B' on reason.

1.2.2 *Enquiry*, Section 4

Suppose we set aside these problems posed by the facts of error and illusion and the question of what it is we are 'really' experiencing. And suppose we accept that we acquire knowledge of matters of fact on the basis of something of which we have direct experience: for instance, that we can make claims about what is happening at some other place on the basis of what we are now hearing reported on the radio, that we can make claims about something that happened in the past on the basis of what we are now remembering or are reading in a history book, or that we can make some claim about what is going to happen—say, that there will be plenty of daffodils in that corner of the courtyard in just a few months' time—on the basis of now noticing the gardeners planting bulbs. If we do suppose these things, and if we also assert the general point that knowledge of any matter of fact can be ultimately traced by some chain of inference back to something which I am now experiencing or remembering, then the question of the nature of this chain of inference is of interest to anyone engaged in enquiry into the scope and limits of knowledge. In Section 4 of the *Enquiry* Hume investigates this question. His remarks have ever since been a rich source of discussion in relation to scepticism, inasmuch as they raise questions about the foundation and justification of inductive inferences. Contemporary discussions of these questions usually take place in the context of the philosophy of science, but Hume raises them about any matter of empirical fact that goes beyond what we are immediately experiencing.

Please now read the whole of Section 4 of the *Enquiry* and note (1) Hume's answer to the question he asks in the third paragraph, beginning, 'What is the nature of that evidence...'; (2) Hume's reasons, as he gives them here, for saying that our knowledge of these matters of fact cannot be founded on reason; (3) any ideas you may have about what sorts of things Hume may be speaking of when he uses the expression 'these *ultimate* springs and principles' in the middle of the penultimate paragraph of Part 1; and (4) how Hume's observations could give rise to scepticism.

Hume argues that we cannot arrive at any truth concerning matters of fact by the method of demonstrative or deductive reasoning, for such reasoning leads to conclusions which, given the truth of the premises, must necessarily be true. The answer to any mathematical problem, if it has been calculated correctly, cannot be otherwise than it is. By contrast, Hume claims, take *any* matter of empirical fact, such as the fact that sun will rise tomorrow, and we can conceive of its being otherwise.

Hume says that when we do go beyond the evidence of our senses to a fact—beyond the letter we are at present reading, say, to the fact that our friend who sent the letter must now be in France—we do so by an inference based on the relation of cause and effect. In this case, we infer that the arrival of the letter was caused by its having been sent by its writer. We make an inference on the basis of having acquired a knowledge of which effects follow from which causes. But such an inference cannot be based on *reason*—by which Hume again means a process of demonstrative reason—for if it were, then we should be able, *prior to all experience of what actually does happen*, to infer what must necessarily have been the cause of something, merely from the immediate experience of that thing. Yet, Hume claims, we can always conceive the cause of any given fact to have been different from what we establish it, by experience, to have been. In terms of the previous example about the daffodils: *if we have had absolutely no experience of plants*, we shall have no reason to suppose that burying a particular sort of object in the ground will result in a blooming daffodil rather than any other plant, or even that it will produce a plant at all. Nor can we deduce, from any statement describing what we see when we see a daffodil, any statement describing what sort of thing has produced that flower.

Hume's view can again be contrasted with that of Descartes. On Descartes' view of knowledge, knowledge of any fact of nature can ultimately be *deduced* from those 'first causes and principles' which he claims to have been established by his method of doubt. Physics is founded on metaphysics—in the strict sense that all knowledge can be ordered according to principles established by metaphysical enquiry. Hume is here combating the idea that there is a necessary connection in nature, discoverable by some rational process, between an effect and its cause. Hume's position can similarly be contrasted with the sort of view which Locke put forward in Book 4 of the *Essay*: Locke's statement that

> I doubt not but if we could discover the figure, size, texture and motion of the minute constituent parts of any two bodies we should know *without trial* several of their operations one upon another, as we do now the properties of a square or a triangle. (*Essay*, IV. iii. 25)

expresses what Hume is denying at several points in Section 4 of the *Enquiry*.

One might, however, put it to Hume that the proposition that the trees will blossom again in the spring can be deduced from some general laws of nature, such as the laws governing the climate in the Northern Hemisphere and its relation to the growth cycle of plants. But then Hume can ask in turn, 'How are these laws and the connections between them to be established, if not by the *experience* of particular instantiations of the laws and of correlations between them?' There is nothing further from which we can infer that these laws *must* hold: all we have are the facts of experience which have no foundation in any necessities. We can discover, *by experience*, that there are certain correlations between various events, but we can never discover why there *must* be such correlations. Even if we attempt to deduce the proposition about the blossoming of the trees from some general principle such as that the future will, in relevant aspects, be conformable to the past, we shall find that this principle must itself be subjected to the test of experience.

In the light of these considerations, then, it seems that any belief concerning matters of fact which goes beyond what we are immediately experiencing, depends upon an *inductive* inference. That is, we make a judgement about something we now see, or expect to see in the future, on the basis of an inference from our previous experience of what we suppose to be the causes or the effects of what we now see. But such an inference provides us with a belief that is, at best, only probable. As Hume remarks, there is a logical gap between the propositions 'I have found that such an object has always been attended with such an effect', and 'I foresee that other objects which are in appearance similar will be attended with similar effects'. Not only do we seem not to know whether the laws of nature which we have established by inductive reasoning are the right ones—that is, whether they are more than a series of coincidences—but it is also unclear, according to Hume (see the third-last paragraph of Part 2 of Section 4), how we can secure ourselves

Problem for Hume's account

against the supposition that the 'secret nature' of bodies may change without any change in their sensible qualities. How do we know, that is, that the law is going to continue to hold in any particular case? If these points are put together, it can seem that our most fundamental beliefs may leave us no better placed as to what to expect than Russell's famous chicken. (See *The Problems of Philosophy*, Chapter 6.)

1.3 SOME GENERAL REMARKS ABOUT SCEPTICISM FOLLOWING FROM HUME'S ARGUMENTS

Here and in section 1.4 I intend to draw some general conclusions from the sorts of arguments we've just been considering, in the light of which we can then set the scene for Moore's and Wittgenstein's treatment of the topic of certainty.

Hume's arguments exploit the fact that we can make a distinction between *the evidence used in support of a judgement*, and *the judgement itself*. For example, I may have a fragment of pottery before me, on the basis of which I claim that a particular community of people lived contemporaneously with, or at some time after, another group of people. Or I predict, on the basis of reading the timetable, that the train will leave at such and such a time; or I calculate that it must be just arriving at York. In each of these cases I make a judgement, on the basis of what I now see before me, about something that happened in the past, something that will happen in the future or something that is now happening in another place. In all these cases I may be wrong. Hume's arguments press the claim that, *no matter how much evidence* I may have in support of such a judgement, it is *always* possible for me to be wrong in assenting to the judgement and for what I claim to be true to be, in fact, false. They press home this claim, *that any statement as to the evidence for some proposition p can be true consistently with the falsity of p*, by concentrating on those cases where there is no gap of time or place. That is, they concentrate on cases in which I am making some claim about what is *now* the case on the basis of what I *now seem* to see. However, as regards what I have isolated as Hume's first argument, the argument from error, Hume is not convinced that this distinction should be pressed to sceptical conclusions. Although he agrees that I can be wrong about what I claim to be true, he maintains that there are ways of resolving the matter. Descartes, on the other hand, insists that we have to find some *general* way of validating this move from evidence to conclusion, if we are not to be reduced to scepticism. But both Hume and Descartes consider that the distinction between evidence and conclusion leads to serious sceptical consequences if it is set up in terms of statements about ideas, or items of immediate experience, and statements about things, or items which are supposed to cause or correspond to such ideas.

If we are to avoid sceptical conclusions, then, it seems that we shall have to find some way of bridging this gap between evidence and conclusion. I'm now going to recast these remarks in terms which will enable us to compare the issues involved in scepticism with Wittgenstein's discussion in *On Certainty*.

The sceptical arguments involve a distinction between, on the one hand, raising a doubt about an issue which can be settled by certain relevant criteria, and, on the other hand, raising doubts about the adequacy of those very criteria themselves. That is, the arguments call into question whether we have any grounds at all for speaking as we do about physical objects like houses and trees, about other minds, about events in the past or about what will happen in the future. For instance, we readily make remarks about how people are feeling, or about what is going to happen; we describe events in history. The sceptical arguments lead us to consider whether or not we are entitled to do so, as all we are ever justified in speaking of is how people behave, or what seems to be happening here and now.

This possibility of doubting the very validity of the grounds for speaking as we do in some specified area of discourse is already familiar from non-philosophical contexts. Attitudes of scepticism or of sheer disbelief are often adopted towards astrology, extrasensory perception, claims that people with supernatural powers exist (such as witches in Medieval Europe), and towards the claims that are involved in religious belief. In these cases doubt is not directed towards some specific claim—whether, say, a particular astrological datum has been correctly arrived at, or whether Widow Grey was responsible for the sickness of the cattle—but is directed against the validity or intelligibility of *any* such claim in the area in question. The doubt questions the adequacy of *any* grounds which might be offered as supporting evidence for such claims.

Philosophical scepticism brings the possibility of this radical form of doubt, quite literally, to our very doors, by applying to the way we talk of trees and houses, other people's feelings, and things which happened in the past or will happen in the future. We are often wrong in claiming to know how someone else feels, but in the normal way we say that there are methods of finding out—for instance, by asking him. But, the first of Hume's arguments urges, how can we be *sure* that we are ever right? And further, in view of the second and third arguments, what justifies us in speaking about other people's feelings at all?

The sceptical arguments, then, seem to demand of us a *justification* for speaking as we do about physical objects, other minds, causal connections or the reality of the past, in much the same way as the religious sceptic demands a justification for talk of God. By the phrase 'speaking as we do', I am referring to such activities as asking questions, making claims and expressing our feelings about situations, objects, people and events. Wittgenstein calls such activities language-games. Putting the matter in Wittgenstein's terms: before we are fully justified in making any particular claim to knowledge about any issue it seems that we shall have to justify the whole language-game in which such a claim has its place.

1.4 SCEPTICISM, IDEALISM AND REALISM

In section 2 of Units 5–6 Stuart Brown stressed the fact that the sorts of issues which we have just been considering raise difficulties for any theory of knowledge in which knowledge is conceived in realist terms: that is, in which knowledge is conceived in terms of a relation between thoughts, beliefs or ideas, on the one hand, and 'reality', the facts, or things which exist quite independently of the knower, on the other. The relation in question can be thought of in various ways: for instance, that beliefs (or, more strictly, the propositions in terms of which beliefs are expressed) *correspond* to the facts; or that ideas *resemble* or *are caused by* objects or properties of objects.

It's difficult, of course, to avoid thinking of the topic in such or similar terms. That someone believes something, or that he is having certain ideas or experiences, is a fact about him; it is a fact about the knowing subject. But what he believes, if his belief is in fact true, is something which can be spoken of and identified independently of any reference to him. It seems obvious, for example, that it can be true that the sun is shining, whether or not anyone believes that it is or is basking in warmth. That is, any truth about the sun—in particular that it exists—is logically independent of any truth about any perceiving subject.

But if the sceptical considerations are right, they pose great difficulties for any claim to know anything about the objects of belief, or indeed for claims that there are any such objects. Scepticism is thus at the root of the division between realism and idealism. For if we are not to give in to scepticism, only two alternatives seem possible. We can either deny that there are two distinct sorts of things between which the sceptical considerations are wedged (e.g. idealism), or we can take up the challenge to give an account of knowledge which bridges the two (realism). There are two assumptions common to both these alternatives, assumptions which will be important to Wittgenstein's approach to the problem. Firstly, both alternatives involve the assumption that it must be possible to specify some indubitable proposition, or class of propositions, which forms the basis of everything we can know. Secondly, they both lead us to revise our concepts of what should be regarded as the proper objects of knowledge.

In this course you've come across three anti-realist positions: in Units 5–6 the idealism of Berkeley and the idealism of Bradley, and in Units 11–13 the position discussed under the name 'verificationism' (which you also studied in its application to problems in the philosophy of mind in Units 23–24, under the title of 'behaviourism'). Berkeley denies that there is any distinction *in being* between ideas and things. The verificationist denies that there is any distinction in *meaning* between conclusive evidence in support of some proposition and the proposition itself. For Berkeley, then, the objects of knowledge are properly describable in terms of our ideas and sensations, and, in denying that we can contrast ideas and sensations with the world, he reduces a claim about what there is to a claim about what we can speak of knowing. Verificationism similarly denies sense to claims about the reality of objects or events which are supposed to lie beyond any possible method of enquiry about them. In terms which will be relevant to a discussion in Unit 32 of Wittgenstein's position *vis-à-vis* these issues, the verificationist position can be called anti-realist in that it accounts for the meaning of a statement in terms of its *assertion or verification conditions* (that is, conditions which are *evidence* for the truth of the statement), whereas a realist position accounts for its meaning in terms of its *truth conditions*. If the meaning of any proposition is to be given in terms of verification (or assertion) conditions, and if there is to be conclusive verification, then, unless we are going to be led into an infinite regress of verifying conditions, there must be some point at which the process of verification comes to an end. There is reason for supposing, then, that both knowledge and meaning must be grounded by reference to some set of basic propositions, propositions which are in some way self-validating. Obvious candidates for propositions which play such a logically basic role in knowledge and meaning are propositions recording the subject's immediate experience. (At this point the verificationist programme *may* be combined with features of Berkeley's programme, in such a way that the meaning of any statement about, say, physical objects is given in terms of whatever ideas or sensations the subject is experiencing.)

In *On Certainty*, as we shall see, Wittgenstein certainly sides with Moore against idealist positions. But some of his remarks, both there and in the *Philosophical Investigations*, have led certain commentators to construe his position along verificationist lines. We shall take this question up at certain later points in these units.

You are by now familiar with the view that Wittgenstein, in his later works, argued against the realist position which he had himself earlier adopted in the *Tractatus*. The *Tractatus* puts forward a realist doctrine of meaning to the extent that it defends the idea that if any proposition is to have definite sense, it must be, or must be equivalent to, a statement or set of statements which correspond directly to the facts of which the world is composed. There is nothing here about any epistemological considerations, but the requirement that there must be objects which are unchanging and eternal if all meaningful propositions are to be given determinate sense is similar in relevant respects, as you may already have noted, to Plato's requirement that the proper objects of knowledge be eternal, unchanging and immutable. More immediately relevant to our interests in *On Certainty*, however, is Russell's programme of logical analysis, which you studied in Units 5–6. This programme insists on many of the same logical conditions that are central to the *Tractatus*, and combines them with an epistemology in which the final constituents of analysis must be terms whose referents can be known for certain if reference to something actually existing is to be secured. Russell's programme, then, is an example of a realist position, in which the sense of items of language is founded on certainty. It is such a position that is the object of the remark Wittgenstein makes at *OC* 477: 'So one must know that the objects whose names one teaches a child by an ostensive definition exist.'

The objects which Russell spoke of in his analysis of knowledge were the objects of *sense experience*. In the first two units of this course, you saw how Descartes put forward the view that the proper objects of knowledge were known by *reason*. Descartes, like Plato, concluded from the sceptical considerations about error and the variability of the ideas of sense, *not* that nothing could be known about the causes of the ideas, but that the objects must be known by some other means: namely, by reason. And, again like Plato, Descartes thought he had a standard of genuine knowledge against which to contrast any mere opinion, the standard provided by the logically indubitable propositions of mathematics and geometry. In the *Regulae*, at the end of Rule II, Descartes tells us that we should 'busy ourselves with no object about which we cannot attain a certitude equal to that of the demonstrations of Mathematics and Geometry'.[1] Now, although it is true that emphasis on the mathematical can distort an account of the limits of human knowledge, there is an important area in which Descartes' emphasis has its place: namely, science. Descartes, indeed, thought of his philosophical work as primarily a methodological foundation for the sciences. Both Descartes and Locke shared the assumption—opposed to that of Hume, as we have seen—that the proper scientific study of the world must be based on truths about the essential nature of things, and that from these truths there could be derived, in a strictly formal sense, truths about the properties and effects of things.

Whether or not Locke, Descartes and Plato are right in their assumption that nature has a rational deductive structure, many people have emphasized that claims to knowledge outside mathematics and the sciences are not only uncertain but are unsystematic and unsupported by any *common method of proof*. In a text-book on psychology, for instance, we read that *scientific* investigation of human behaviour can show us that 'what was once a matter of belief, prejudice and presumption based on personal experience, is now knowledge based on evidence'.[2] Behind such a claim lies, I think, the observation that scientific method can be seen, in part, as an *objective and systematic* method of isolating, quantifying and comparing the variables in any enquiry. Science presents us with an objective picture of the world in the

---

[1] Cambridge ed., page 5.
[2] Wright, D., *The Psychology of Moral Behaviour*, Penguin, 1971.

sense that it provides us with a method of discovering facts which is not dependent on the variable viewpoint or interest of any particular observer; and one reason for this is that the objects of enquiry are confined to those things which can be quantified and measured. The Galilean system, for example, which so impressed Descartes and Locke, takes the objects of scientific enquiry to be the mathematical properties of objects not immediately present to the senses.

This distinction, however, between the world as it is experienced and the world as the object of scientific discovery, gives rise to a paradox. I'll remind you of the problem as it was presented by Stuart Brown in Units 11–13 (page 8)—a discussion which itself takes off from the way the issue was first discussed in Units 3–4:

> In Units 3–4, Susan Khin Zaw explained how the new science of the seventeenth century disclosed, or was thought to have disclosed, a gulf between the world of common experience and the world of physics. The science of the time seemed to be giving content to the idea that things as they really are differ from what they appear to us to be. What we experience, it seemed, is only the effect of the objects investigated by science, and the ideas those objects produce in us need bear no resemblance to anything in the objects themselves. There is nothing, for example, in objects themselves resembling the colours, tastes, and smells which are part of the world of common experience. To be sure, there is something about the objects in virtue of which we experience them as having the colours, tastes and smells we are tempted to attribute to them. But they themselves are not coloured, neither do they have any taste or smell. Such qualities are, as Locke put it, 'nothing in the objects themselves but powers to produce various sensations in us ... by the bulk, figure, texture, and motion of their insensible parts'. (*Essay*, II. viii. 10) On such a view the world seems to be, as Susan Khin Zaw puts it, 'no longer the familiar clutter which we can see and feel and smell and hear, but an alien and remote assemblage of particles ...' (Units 3–4, p. 18). Such a view is paradoxical, since it at once casts doubt on whether the senses provide us with the real truth about the physical world yet, at the same time, is itself founded on the results of experiments and to that extent based on the evidence of the senses.

The view of knowledge involved in this picture of science is a realist one inasmuch as the establishment of truth or falsity is regarded as a matter of there being an independent reality with which one's investigations, measurements and statements can accord or conflict. It is a questionable view only inasmuch as it also involves the claims that the ways in which we classify, calculate and describe in the sciences are the right ones, because only they accurately reflect facts about things, and that these facts are independent of our language and ways of thought. This view, and these claims, will be relevant to certain remarks in *On Certainty*, for two reasons. First, they raise the question whether there is any sense in which the application of any method of enquiry can be regarded as entirely independent of facts about human principles of organizing the data of enquiry, or of facts about human perception. Secondly, they may seem to provide us with a standard for judging the rationality or validity of any belief which plays a fundamental role in people's lives—i.e., a belief which is, according to the standards of science, just false.

1.5   SUMMARY

Sceptical considerations exploit the possibility of a doubt which arises when we observe that it is logically possible for any judgement based on evidence to be false, no matter how conclusive we suppose our evidence to be. That is, such considerations present us with the *logical possibility of doubt* in even the most mundane of cases, and lead us to suppose that even talk of trees and houses involves some element of inference.

This question of the logical possibility of doubt is one to which many of Wittgenstein's remarks in *On Certainty* are addressed. It is the topic of section 3 of these units.

In order to avoid sceptical conclusions about the scope of knowledge, we apparently have to meet the challenge to *justify* our statements and beliefs by showing that they can somehow be derived from a proposition, or set of propositions, which is indubitable. There is much disagreement about the actual foundations specified and their role in any system of knowledge. One common feature of candidates for the role of such propositions, however, offered by both Descartes and Russell, is that a proposition is certain only if it is not based on evidence at all: that is, if it is in some way self-guaranteeing.

Questions about the foundations of knowledge and meaning are also directly relevant to many of Wittgenstein's remarks concerning the sorts of things which Moore claimed to know. We'll look at Moore's claims in section 2, and take up the issues of the foundations of knowledge and meaning from Wittgenstein's point of view in section 4.

2 G. E. MOORE AND CLAIMS TO KNOW OR BELIEVE THAT CERTAIN THINGS ARE TRUE

2.1 MOORE'S EXAMPLES

In his memoir of Wittgenstein, Norman Malcolm tells us how he and Wittgenstein had discussed some of the things which G. E. Moore had said and written on the topic of certainty. In particular they talked about

> Moore's insistence that it is a correct use of language for him to say, when holding one of his hands before him, 'I *know* that this is a hand'; or to say, while pointing at a tree a few feet away, 'I *know* for *certain* that this is a *tree*! (*Ludwig Wittgenstein: A Memoir*, Oxford, page 87)

The example of someone claiming to know that 'this is a tree' is a recurring one throughout *On Certainty*, and the example of someone claiming to know that 'this is a hand' is the example which begins the notes in the book. Moore discusses the second example in two papers: 'A Defence of Common Sense', which originally appeared in 1925, and 'Proof of an External World', which was a lecture he gave in 1939. These papers, and a third paper called 'Certainty', which originally appeared in 1941, have all been published together in Moore's *Philosophical Papers* (Allen and Unwin, 1959), which I shall abbreviate as *PhP*. All three papers are well worth reading as an independent treatment of the topic of knowledge and certainty, but Wittgenstein's interest in them lies primarily in the nature of the things which Moore enumerates as examples of things he knows, and in the fact that Moore said that he knew them. Consequently, I shall mention or discuss only certain passages from Moore's papers which I judge to relate directly to the remarks in *OC*, and use them to develop some general points about knowledge and belief arising from those remarks.

Moore's paper 'Certainty' begins by listing a number of things which Moore goes on to claim that, at the time of speaking, he knew for certain to be true.

> I am at present, as you can all see, in a room and not in the open air; I am standing up, and not either sitting or lying down; I have clothes on, and am not absolutely naked; I am speaking in a fairly loud voice, and am not either singing or whispering or keeping quite silent; I have in my hand some sheets of paper with writing on them; there are a good many other people in the same room in which I am; and there are windows in that wall and a door in this one. (*PhP*, page 225)

Moore says of these things that they are all instances of the class of propositions which imply the existence of an external world, and are as good test cases as could have been chosen for deciding whether or not the existence of anything external to the mind can be known for certain (*PhP*, pp. 242–44). They are, he says, test cases for those arguments 'which have sometimes been alleged to show that nobody ever has known for certain anything about a world external to his mind'. His example of such an argument is our familiar one from dreaming:

> Suppose I say now: 'I know for certain that I am standing up; it is absolutely certain that I am; there is not the smallest chance that I am not.' Many philosophers would say: 'You are wrong: you do not know that you are standing up; it is *not* absolutely certain that you are; there is *some* chance, though perhaps only a very small one, that you are not.' And one argument

which has been used as an argument in favour of saying this, is an argument in the course of which the philosopher who used it would assert: 'You do not know for certain that you are not dreaming; it is not absolutely certain that you are not; there is *some* chance, though perhaps only a very small one, that you are.' And from this, that I do not know for certain that I am not dreaming, it is supposed to follow that I do not know for certain that I am standing up. It is argued: If it is not certain that you are not dreaming, then it is not certain that you are standing up. (*PhP*, page 245)

Moore goes on to discuss this argument, though in a way which he himself felt to be unsatisfactory. His discussion, however, involves a significant observation which he had made about the examples listed at the beginning of the paper: namely, that the propositions are all alike in being *contingent* propositions. But from this, he claims, it does *not* follow that any one of them, at the time at which he said it, could *possibly* be false.

Now, as is apparent from the discussion of section 1, the sceptical arguments get their force from exploiting the fact that a given proposition is contingent, and so *might have been* false. Their conclusion is that, for all we know, it could *actually be* false. Moore's argument is a denial of this:

> From the fact that some proposition is contingent, it does not follow that it is possible that the proposition is false, for this implies that I do not know that it is true. Whereas, *I do know*. (*PhP*, page 234)

But this is, of course, the very point at issue. Wittgenstein, as we shall see in section 3, agrees with Moore's claim here; but he denies that the mere assertion that one does know the things in question is any kind of argument. (See, for example, *OC* 521 and 15–16.)

Moore's argument, however, exhibits an important and fundamental difference of approach—a difference he shares with Wittgenstein—from that of the philosophers who are impressed by the sceptical considerations. Descartes, for instance, as we have seen, approached the question of knowledge as follows: we have first to establish authoritative standards or principles of knowledge, and we can then use these standards to assess whether any claim to knowledge is indeed a genuine claim. This procedure may lead us radically to revise our ideas about the sorts of things we can know. Moore, however, proceeds the other way around: he begins from examples of things we know, and takes these as unrevisable standards against which to measure any account of knowledge. It is in this sense that Moore's arguments are said to be defending 'common sense'.

In his paper 'A Defence of Common Sense', Moore likewise begins by listing propositions which he claims to know with certainty to be true:

> I begin, then, with my list of truisms, every one of which (in my own opinion) I *know*, with certainty, to be true.
> There exists at present a living human body, which is *my* body. This body was born at a certain time in the past, and has existed continuously ever since, though not without undergoing changes; it was, for instance, much smaller when it was born, and for some time afterwards, than it is now. Ever since it was born, it has been either in contact with or not far from the surface of the earth; and, at every moment since it was born, there have also existed many other things, having shape and size in three dimensions (in the same familiar sense in which it has), from which it has been *at various distances* (in the familiar sense in which it is now at a distance both from that mantelpiece and from that bookcase, and at a greater distance from the bookcase than it is from the mantelpiece); also there have (very often, at all events) existed some other things of this kind with which it was *in contact* (in the familiar sense in which it

is now in contact with the pen I am holding in my right hand and with some of the clothes I am wearing). Among the things which have, in this sense, formed part of its environment (i.e. have been either in contact with it, or at *some* distance from it, however *great*) there have, at every moment since its birth, been large numbers of other living human bodies, each of which has, like it, (*a*) at some time been born, (*b*) continued to exist from some time after birth, (*c*) been, at every moment of its life after birth, either in contact with or not far from the surface of the earth; and many of these bodies have already died and ceased to exist. But the earth had existed also for many years before my body was born; and for many of these years, also, large numbers of human bodies had, at every moment, been alive upon it; and many of these bodies had died and ceased to exist before it was born. (*PhP*, page 34)

Facts such as those he enumerates here Moore describes as physical facts, and it is his contention in this paper that there is no good reason to suppose, in the case of *every* physical fact, that it could not have been a fact unless some corresponding statement describing a mental fact had also been true. 'The earth has existed for many years past' is an example of a physical fact about which this is true. Moore, then, is disagreeing with those philosophers (on page 51 of *PhP* he cites Berkeley as an example) who hold that the objects mentioned in any of his examples of physical facts—my body, the mantelpiece, the world—are either 'ideas' or 'constituted by ideas', and who claim that no object can possibly exist without being perceived.

Moore's anti-idealist position here is based on his claim that there is a clear distinction to be made between the *truth* of propositions 'which assert the existence of material things' (as he describes them on page 53), and the *proper analysis* of them. When he first makes this point (on page 37), he does so in terms of the *meaning* of the propositions. He writes:

> Such an expression as 'The earth has existed for many years past' is the very type of an unambiguous expression, the meaning of which we all understand. Anyone who takes a contrary view must, I suppose, be confusing the question whether we understand its meaning (which we all certainly do) with the entirely different question whether we *know what it means*, in the sense that we are able to *give a correct analysis* of its meaning. The question what is the correct analysis of *the* proposition meant *on any occasion* (for, of course, as I insisted in defining (2), a different proposition is meant at every different time at which the expression is used) by 'The earth has existed for many years past' is, it seems to me, a profoundly difficult question, and one to which, as I shall presently urge, no one knows the answer.

From the context of this paper alone, though, it isn't clear exactly what this distinction of meaning is, or how it connects with knowledge. From the fact that he here says that a different proposition is meant each time some expression is used I shall assume that by the 'meaning' of a proposition Moore means that to which the expression refers on each occasion of its use. On page 53 he gives a further account of what he means by the analysis of a proposition:

> It seems to me quite evident that the question how propositions of the type I have just given are to be analysed, depends on the question how propositions of another and simpler type are to be analysed. I know, at present, that I am perceiving a human hand, a pen, a sheet of paper, etc.; and it seems to me that I cannot know how the proposition 'Material things exist' is to be analysed, until I know how, in certain respects, these simpler propositions are to be analysed. But even these are not simple enough. It seems to me quite evident that my knowledge that I am now perceiving a human hand is a deduction from a pair of propositions simpler still—propositions which I can only express in the form 'I am perceiving *this*' and '*This* is a human hand'. It

is the analysis of propositions of the latter kind which seems to me to present such great difficulties, while nevertheless the whole question as to the *nature* of material things obviously depends upon their analysis.

So from this, we can know whether material objects such as hands or the world exist, but we cannot be certain how to give an account of what such things consist of—that is, of their *nature*. It might be thought that the question of their nature was a question for science, but Moore is quite definitely not thinking along these lines:

> Two things only seem to me to be quite certain about the analysis of such propositions (and even with regard to these I am afraid some philosophers would differ from me) namely that whenever I know, or judge, such a proposition to be true, (1) there is always some *sense-datum* about which the proposition in question is a proposition—some sense-datum which is *a* subject (and, in a certain sense, the principal or ultimate subject) of the proposition in question, and (2) that, nevertheless, *what* I am knowing or judging to be true about this sense-datum is not (in general) that it is *itself* a hand, or a dog, or the sun, etc. etc., as the case may be. (*PhP*, page 54)

And on page 55 he says that he holds it to be quite certain that one does not *directly* perceive a hand, but that one perceives something which is a *representative* of it. It seems, then, that giving a correct analysis of the meaning of a proposition such as 'This is a hand' must be a matter of stating the sorts of object to which the proposition is directly or ultimately referring.

But how does this possibility of analysis relate to the question whether I know the proposition to be true? Well, Moore says that in the case of most of the propositions which he began by enumerating, it is obvious that he did not know them directly but knew them only because he knew other things which were evidence for them. Yet in order to be right in saying he knew them, he need not necessarily know what this evidence was or is (page 44). And in the passage I quoted above from page 53, he says that his knowledge that he was perceiving a human hand was *deduced* from other propositions, namely 'I am perceiving *this*', and 'This is a human hand'. So: we do not, according to Moore, have to be able to give an account of what exactly 'this' refers to in those situations; but we must be able to know such things as 'This is a human hand' if other statements about material objects are to be known to be true.

In his paper 'Proof of an External World', Moore again states that his knowledge that there are material things—in particular, that these are hands—is something that he knows because it can be deduced from 'simple' propositions. In fact, he says, this knowledge enables him to *prove* the existence of 'external things' such as hands. (The first remark of *On Certainty* can be read in connection with Moore's project here.) On page 146 Moore writes:

> I can prove now, for instance, that two human hands exist. How? By holding up my two hands, and saying, as I make a certain gesture with the right hand, 'Here is one hand', and adding, as I make a certain gesture with the left, 'and here is another'. And if, by doing this, I have proved *ipso facto* the existence of external things, you will all see that I can also do it now in numbers of other ways: there is no need to multiply examples.

He does not use the term 'proof' lightly, but goes on to say:

> Of course, it would not have been a proof unless three conditions were satisfied; namely (1) unless the premiss which I adduced as proof of the ·

conclusion was different from the conclusion I adduced it to prove; (2) unless the premiss which I adduced was something which I *knew* to be the case, and not merely something which I believed but which was by no means certain, or something which, though in fact true, I did not know to be so; and (3) unless the conclusion did really follow from the premiss. But all these three conditions were in fact satisfied by my proof. (1) The premiss which I adduced in proof was quite certainly different from the conclusion, for the conclusion was merely 'Two human hands exist at this moment'; but the premiss was something far more specific than this—something which I expressed by showing you my hands, making certain gestures, and saying the words 'Here is one hand, and here is another'. It is quite obvious that the two were different, because it is quite obvious that the conclusion might have been true, even if the premiss had been false. In asserting the premiss I was asserting much more than I was asserting in asserting the conclusion. (2) I certainly did at the moment *know* that which I expressed by the combination of certain gestures with saying the words 'There is one hand and here is another'. I *knew* that there was one hand in the place indicated by combining a certain gesture with my first utterance of 'here' and that there was another in the different place indicated by combining a certain gesture with my second utterance of 'here'. How absurd it would be to suggest that I did not know it, but only believed it, and that perhaps it was not the case! You might as well suggest that I do not know that I am now standing up and talking—that perhaps after all I'm not, and that it's not quite certain that I am! And finally (3) it is quite certain that the conclusion did follow from the premiss. This is as certain as it is that if there is one hand here and another here *now*, then it follows that there are two hands in existence *now*.

The second condition of his having proved that there exist two hands is that the proof was based on a premise which he *knew* to be true. He states this premise as: 'That which I expressed by the combination of certain gestures with saying the words, "there is one hand and here is another"'. Now a little further on in the paper he points out that he is

> perfectly well aware that, in spite of all that I have said, many philosophers will still feel that I have not given any satisfactory proof of the point in question. (page 148)

Such philosophers would demand proof of the *premise*, 'Here is one hand', before agreeing that he had proved the existence of external things. The sceptic, however, might agree that, *if* Moore could justify his claim to know that 'Here is one hand', then 'he would grant Moore all the rest'. (Cf. the first remark of *On Certainty*.)

Moore quite rightly says that what such philosophers really want is something like a general statement as to how any proposition of this sort may be proved. In reply to this, he completely agrees that he has not given a proof of his *premise*, but he says that he does not believe that any proof could be given. For in order to give a proof, he says, 'I should need to prove for one thing, as Descartes pointed out, that I am not now dreaming' (page 149). And he goes on to say that 'I have conclusive evidence that I am awake: but that is a very different thing from being able to prove it' (page 149).

So, on Moore's account, proving something to be true is different from having conclusive evidence for it. Moore does say, however, that in some cases *what might be called* a proof of such propositions can be obtained:

> Of course, in some cases what might be called a proof of propositions which seem like these can be got. If one of you suspected that one of my hands was artificial he might be said to get a proof of my proposition 'Here's one hand,

and here's another', by coming up and examining the suspected hand close up, perhaps touching and pressing it, and so establishing that it really was a human hand. (page 149)

Why do you think Moore says that this is only 'what might be called' a proof?

I think the answer to this is that he accepts the strictures implicit in the sceptical arguments as to what is to count as a proof. Something is proved only if it is arrived at as the conclusion of a deductive argument from premises which are known. There is, on this view, only one kind of proof, namely that used in the demonstrative methods of geometry and formal logic. Moore claims on this basis that he has proved the conclusion, 'There exist at least two external objects', from the premise, 'Here is one hand and here is another'. But 'Here is one hand' has not itself been proved. The sceptical arguments, which suggest that it is always conceivable that such a judgement may be wrong, are based on the fact that the judgement cannot be derived in this strict sense from premises which the sceptic might acknowledge as more certain, namely premises about 'sense-data'. (From what Moore says about sense-data, however, a sense-datum is not obviously a constituent of what he would call a mental fact, and statements about sense-data are no more certain than are statements about things like hands.) (Cf. again *OC* 1.) Moore agrees with his opponents, then, as to the nature of proof, but staunchly maintains that many things can be known which can't be proved. In terms of his distinction between proof and conclusive evidence, examining the suspected hand by touching and pressing is something he will acknowledge as conclusive evidence, but not as a proof. So much the worse for this standard of proof as a criterion of knowledge, he concludes.

We'll see later, in section 4, that although Wittgenstein is in agreement with Moore's conclusion here, his reasons for rejecting the idea that knowledge is only to be understood in terms of one method of proof are very different. And in contrast with both Moore and the sceptic, Wittgenstein rejects the intelligibility of asking for a proof of the external world. But Wittgenstein's immediate interest, in *On Certainty*, lies in the fact that in all three of his papers Moore has based his opposition to the sceptic and the idealist on his claim to *know* that certain things are true.

[handwritten margin note: Moore — he claims — to know certain things are true.]

2.2   WITTGENSTEIN'S CRITICISMS OF MOORE'S CLAIMS TO KNOW

At *OC* 6 Wittgenstein asks the question: can one enumerate what one knows in the way Moore did? His answer is that he doesn't believe you can, 'straight off, like that'. There is a passage from the *Blue Book*, however, in which he seems to offer the opposite answer. On *BB* page 20 he writes, 'When Socrates asks the question, "What is knowledge", he does not even regard it as a *preliminary* answer to enumerate cases of knowledge'; the tone and context suggest that Wittgenstein does think, there, that enumerating cases of knowledge would be a preliminary answer. So we want to know the answers to two questions: has Wittgenstein changed his mind on this matter, and, more importantly, what are his reasons for saying what he does, in either place?

The passage preceding this sentence in the *Blue Book* reads as follows: 'The idea that in order to get clear about the meaning of a general term one had to find the common elements in all its applications has shackled philosophical investigation; for it has not only led to no result, but has also made the philosopher dismiss as irrelevant the concrete cases, which alone could have helped him to understand, the usage of the general term' (*BB*, pp. 19–20). So here Wittgenstein is advocating that we should proceed with regard for the way any claim to, or denial of, knowledge is actually made *and* that this can be done by enumerating cases of things known. In *On Certainty*, as we shall see in 2.2.2 below, Wittgenstein still thinks that paying close attention to the way claims to knowledge are actually made and substantiated is the way to proceed in a philosophical enquiry about knowledge, and it is his adherence to this procedure and what it implies for any account of meaning which is the pivot of much of the argument in the book. In *On Certainty*, however, he thinks that enumerating what you know is *not* a preliminary part of this procedure. For if you attempt to make an enumeration, he says, 'the expression "I know" gets misused. And through this misuse a queer and extremely important mental state seems to be revealed' (*OC* 6). So we want to know, more specifically: (1) how does he think Moore misuses 'I know', and (2) what can we learn about knowledge from what Wittgenstein regards as more correct cases of how 'I know' is used?

2.2.1 Knowledge and belief as mental states

Please now read the first twenty-four sections, section 128 and sections 179–81 of *On Certainty*, and note down your answer to the question arising from *OC* 6: how does Wittgenstein think that Moore misuses 'I know'? Sections 12–13, 21 and 179 are particularly relevant.

Wittgenstein thinks that Moore uses 'I know' as though he were insisting to the sceptic that the things he claimed to know must in fact be true *because* he, Moore, felt certain, or thought he was in a state of knowledge, about those things. *OC* 128 brings out the two points which Wittgenstein thinks are involved here: firstly, that Moore regards 'I know' as a statement describing his state of mind, and so, arguably, as a statement which is not subject to doubt; secondly, that Moore places a false emphasis on the fact that from saying 'I know it is so', I can infer that it is so. *If* it were correct to regard 'I know...' as a report of my state of mind about which I could not be mistaken, and *since* I can infer from 'I know...' that 'it is so', *then* that would be an extremely important mental state (*OC* 6). For it would be a state which would guarantee the truth of whatever is being claimed.

I'll now go into this question in some detail, in order to bring out some points of comparison between knowledge and belief. As I mentioned earlier, Norman Malcolm has recorded a conversation he had with Wittgenstein on the topic of certainty, concerning in particular some of the things which Moore had said. Malcolm reports Wittgenstein as saying:

> There is a tendency to think of knowledge as a *mental state*...Mental states, such as anxiety and pain, have degrees. Certainty also has degrees, e.g. 'How certain are you?' Since certainty has degrees we are helped to have the idea that knowledge is a mental state.

> Moore would like to stare at a house that is only 20 feet away and say, with a peculiar intonation, 'I know that there's a house!' He does this because he wants to produce in himself the feeling of knowing. He wants to exhibit knowing for certain to himself. In this way he has the idea that he is replying to the sceptical philosopher who claims that everyday examples of knowing

that there is a dog in the backyard, or that the neighbour's house is on fire, are not really or strictly knowledge, are not knowledge in the highest degree. It is as if someone had said 'You don't really feel pain when you are pinched' and Moore then pinched himself in order to feel the pain, and thus prove to himself that the other is wrong. Moore treats the sentence 'I know so & so' like the sentence 'I have a pain.' The criterion that he knows that so & so will be that he *says* that he does. (Malcolm, pp. 87–88)

From your work in previous units in the second half of this course, you will probably be able to anticipate that Wittgenstein wishes to discourage the desire to 'exhibit *knowing for certain* to himself'. This is the point of *OC* 601, and the general point behind *OC* 38. However, there is an argument specifically directed against knowing's being a mental state, in a paragraph which I omitted from the quotation from Malcolm's notes above:

> Now I am supposed to know my own mental states. If I say I have a certain mental state and do not have it, then I have told a lie. But I can say that I know so & so and it can turn out that so & so is false; but it doesn't follow that I lied. Therefore, knowing is not a mental state. (page 87)

What does follow, if so and so is false, is that I was wrong in saying that I *knew* (*OC* 12, 21). This is not the case, however, with *belief* or with *being certain*. Contrary to what Wittgenstein says at *OC* 8, there does seem to be a difference between knowing and being certain, in that, even if I turn out to be wrong about what I feel certain about, I would not be wrong in thinking that I was certain (cf. *OC* 30). Following the thought of *OC* 8, one reason why it might be forbidden to say 'I know' in a court of law might be to remind the jury that it doesn't follow that someone is telling the truth *about what he claims to know*, from the fact that he is truthfully *claiming to know it*. As regards the reference to *Wilhelm Meister* mentioned in this passage, it could have been said to the person who claimed to know: 'For all your certainty, you didn't *know*'. However, the point of the denial of a difference between saying 'I know' and saying 'I am certain' is to show that saying that I know no more guarantees the truth of what I claim to know than does saying that I am certain. At *OC* 179 Wittgenstein contrasts 'I know' with 'I believe' and says that 'I believe...' has subjective truth but 'I know...' does not. This follows on from the preceding section, in which 'I know' is contrasted with 'I am in pain' and in which Wittgenstein accuses Moore of regarding 'I know' as an utterance as little subject to doubt as 'I am in pain'. What is meant by 'subjective truth' here is, I think, simply that 'I believe...' is a truth about the subject, i.e. the person who is saying he believes. In *OC* 180 Wittgenstein gives what seems to be an alternative way of putting the point, namely that 'I believe' is an 'expression'.

Now the word 'pain' can be used in giving verbal expression to my state or feeling. There would be a danger, however, in viewing the expression of a belief on the same lines. Bearing in mind the contrast that was made in Units 23–24, section 4.1, between belief and feeling, why do you think it would be misleading to assimilate the two too easily?

The concept of belief cannot be understood merely as the expression of a state of mind, as though it were the expression of the way one feels towards an idea. In Units 23–24, Section 4.1, this issue was discussed with reference to Hume, who does seem to have thought of belief in terms of some added psychological feature of an idea. What an account such as Hume's overlooks is that belief has a kind of complexity, as it was put in Units 23–24, which has no counterpart in the case of pain. Let me remind you of what Oswald Hanfling said in the earlier units:

> Belief has a kind of complexity which has no counterpart in the case of pain. The statement that one has a pain is 'complete' in a way in which the statement that one has a belief is not. Belief necessarily has an object: there must be something *that* I believe. And similarly with thought, attention and the like; but not with a sensation such as pain. It might be thought that a counterpart in the case of pain is its cause. It is true that one often mentions the cause of the pain. But this is not necessarily so. 'I have a pain, I don't know what from' makes sense; whereas 'I have a belief' cannot be left uncompleted in this way. (Units 23–24, page 41).

In the case of belief the 'object' which Oswald Hanfling speaks of (and which, of course, is more akin to a grammatical object than to a physical object) is something which can be true or false. I believe, for instance, that my cat is pregnant again, and it is either true or false that she is. This feature of belief involves the important point that a person is answerable for his beliefs: I should be able to say what justifies me in believing what I do, i.e. I should be able to give reasons. So my answer to the question why it is misleading to assimilate a state of belief to a state of pain or feeling is that belief is a state of mind which is amenable to *reason* in the way in which most aches, pains and sensations are not. (I say 'most' here, because psychosomatic pains may well be amenable to reason, but this is, significantly, only in so far as they are connected in the sufferer, either consciously or unconsciously, with some cognitive attitude.)

Having introduced the notion of the complexity of belief, we can now turn to that fact about the use of 'I know...' which, according to Wittgenstein, misled Moore: namely, the fact that I can infer 'It is so' from 'I know it to be so'. For both knowledge and belief are essentially directed at truth. Belief, as it were, aims at truth, whereas knowledge purports to have arrived at it.

In saying of someone that he knows or believes something it seems possible to distinguish two questions: (i) a question about the person making the claim—does he in fact know or believe what he claims to know or believe? and (ii) a question about what he claims to know or believe—is it true? We can then ask whether the relation between these two questions is the same in the cases of knowledge and belief.

Let's take the case of belief first. The two questions can be answered independently, inasmuch as whether or not it is true that I believe something is not dependent on the truth or falsity of what I claim to believe. Yet there is a peculiarity which arises in a first-person assertion of belief: *I* cannot claim to believe something and yet also say that what I believe is false. There may seem to be a paradox here, if you think that what is true of the relation between the fact that someone believes *p*, and the fact that *p*, ought to be just the same whether I state the fact or someone else does. In fact, this has gone down in the literature as Moore's paradox, for it was Moore who explicitly presented it.

In *PI* II, x Wittgenstein discusses the paradox. I leave it to you as an exercise to see whether, and if so how, he presents the elements involved in the paradox in such a way that it disappears. I shall not offer any considerations of my own with which you can compare yours. I *suggest*, though, that you read very critically the statement in quotation marks which begins the sixth paragraph on page 190, especially in connection with the photograph analogy which follows it. What is the relevance, do you think, of the fact that 'I must also be able to say that the photograph is a good one'?

And a warning about the passage beginning 'This is how I think of it...' at the bottom of page 191: don't suppose that Wittgenstein is claiming that this *is* the right way of thinking of the problem. For if it were, it would appear to be necessary, in order to recognize for myself that I believe something, that I 'take notice of myself as others do, listen to myself talking, etc', although, as Wittgenstein recognizes, there seems to be room in *some* cases for saying that I discovered what I believed through realization of what I was doing or saying.

In the case of knowledge, the two questions which we distinguished on page 29 are not independent of one another. A person is right in claiming that he knows something only if what he claims to know is in fact true, and so, *if* he does know, then it follows that what he knows is true. As far as the first-person case is concerned, once again, from the fact that I think I am right in saying 'I know' that something is the case, *I* can infer it is so. But, of course, from the fact that I say I know, no-one else is entitled to infer that it is so, unless he has reason to believe that I am a reliable authority on the matter. Wittgenstein makes these points specifically, at *OC* 11–16. Moore, then, according to Wittgenstein, has overlooked the fact that whether I do know something, or merely think I do, has to be shown by, for example, a demonstration that I am not mistaken.

At *OC* 415 Wittgenstein writes:

> And in fact, isn't the use of the word 'know' as a predominantly philosophical word altogether wrong? If 'know' has this interest, why not 'being certain'? Apparently because it would be too subjective. But isn't 'know' *just* as subjective? Isn't one misled simply by the grammatical peculiarity that 'p' follows from 'I know p'?

Assuming that his answers to these questions are 'yes' in each case, then they go against what he said at *OC* 179, that 'I know p' does not have subjective truth. However, as we have seen, Wittgenstein's point at 179 was to emphasize that a claim to knowledge, unlike a claim to belief, is not independent of the truth of what is being claimed. Here, at 415, his saying that a claim to knowledge does have subjective truth connects with the remark that the use of the word 'know' as a predominantly philosophical word is wrong. That is, the expression 'I know' cannot be used in the way Moore tried to use it, as part of a philosophical argument, in order to counter the sceptical arguments or the claims of the idealist. (Cf. *OC* 482.) For 'an assurance from a reliable man that he *knows* cannot contribute anything'. (I have taken this remark from *OC* 21, which summarizes the points we have made in this section.) 'I know that it is so' is subjective in the sense that it involves a claim about the judging subject in the way in which the assertion 'It is so' does not. (Cf. also *OC* 593.)

In using 'I know', Moore has left himself open to the philosopher who says 'I believe it merely strikes you as if you know it' (cf. *OC* 487–490). For Moore's remarks were directed at the idealist who denies the existence of things in the world external to the mind. At *OC* 19 Wittgenstein makes a distinction between a practical doubt and a philosophical doubt. Moore's statement of knowledge could be appropriate to the removal of a practical doubt, but the idealist is dealing, as Wittgenstein puts it at *OC* 19, with 'a further doubt *behind* the practical one'. This distinction between a practical and a philosophical doubt is very similar to the distinction, made in section 1 of these units, between doubts which can in principle be settled by the ordinary relevant criteria and doubts which call those very criteria into question.

(Wittgenstein gives an example of a practical doubt at *OC* 20 and also at *OC* 259.) The situation envisaged at the beginning of *OC* 19 is one in which there is some practical doubt about a hand—perhaps there's some confusion about something seen in a mirror in a dim light. Moore's insistence that he knows that there is a hand, though it could well be appropriate in such a situation, does nothing to meet those doubts which the sceptical or idealist arguments trade upon. You might compare Wittgenstein's remarks here with his discussion in the *Blue Book* (pp. 48–49) of the way the realist skips the difficulties which his adversaries see.

Wittgenstein's view of Moore's use of 'I know', then, is that, in the context of Moore's papers, it does nothing to meet the difficulties which Moore's adversaries emphasize, and that Moore was misled into thinking it did have some argumentative point by misconstruing 'I know' as a report about his state of mind concerning what he claimed to know—a state of mind which would guarantee its truth.

2.2.2 Wittgenstein's remarks on the correct use of 'I know'

At *OC* 32 Wittgenstein says that it is not a matter of Moore's *knowing* that there is a hand, but rather that we should not understand if he were to say that he might be wrong. As we have just seen, whether or not someone is right in claiming to know something depends, according to Wittgenstein, on whether or not we can show, for one thing, that he has not made a mistake. But, Wittgenstein asks, in the case of the sorts of things which Moore instances, what would it be like to make a mistake? (He also makes this point at *OC* 17.) At *OC* 243 he holds that one says 'I know' when one has compelling grounds by appeal to which the truth of what one claims to know can be demonstrated. And at *OC* 483 he actually gives several examples of the correct use of the expression 'I know': they are all cases of being able to say *how* one knows (cf. also *OC* 550). From all this we can make two general points: that Wittgenstein sees a claim to knowledge as *essentially connected with the evidence which can be given in support or confirmation of what one knows*, and that this claim is, in turn, something *about which it is possible to be mistaken*. These views mark Wittgenstein off quite radically from those philosophers who try to make a clear separation at some ultimate level between knowledge and evidence and who try to establish truths about which one can be infallible.

At *OC* 504 Wittgenstein extends his claim that whether someone knows something is a matter of whether the evidence backs him up or not, with the remark: 'for to say one knows one has a pain means nothing'. This in itself is merely a re-assertion of the position he had stated in the *Philosophical Investigations* (Part 1, para. 246 and Part 2, pp. 220 ff.). There was a detailed discussion of this point in Units 20–22, sections 3.6–3.9, where Wittgenstein's remarks about saying 'I know I am in pain' are summed up as follows:

> In these passages [from *PI*] Wittgenstein is undermining a long tradition of philosophical endeavour ('a whole cloud of philosophy condensed into a drop of grammar', p. 222). The endeavour has been to find *some* knowledge which is immune from doubt. Without such a basis, it has been held, *all* our knowledge might really be error. Descartes thought he had found such knowledge when he stated his doctrine of clear and distinct ideas and when he propounded the *cogito*. Nearer to our time, G. E. Moore proposed a number of statements as being immune from doubt and as being, in that way, really 'safe' items of knowledge. (pp. 30–31).

One of the passages Oswald Hanfling refers to reads:

> It is correct to say 'I know what you are thinking', and wrong to say 'I know

what I am thinking'. (A whole cloud of philosophy condensed into a drop of grammar.) (*PI* II, xi, page 222)

Now even those who otherwise sympathize with many of Wittgenstein's views have thought that he was being too severe, or was being perverse, in maintaining that it is incorrect to say such things as 'I know I am in pain' or 'I know I have two hands'. (See, for example, pp. 130–32 of the article 'How to Read Wittgenstein' by Renford Bambrough in the R.I.P. volume *Understanding Wittgenstein*.) What has to be taken into account, however, is that Wittgenstein is denying something quite specific when he denies that 'I know I am in pain' is a correct example of what one can be said to know: namely, that if it is used as a point of argument in a philosophical account of knowledge, it does not provide an example of something known against which most other claims can be measured and can be seen to fall short. In *PI*, Part II (page 221) he repeats the point that one says 'I know' where one can find out, and continues:

> If you bring up against me the case of people's saying 'But I must know if I am in pain!' . . . you should consider the occasion and purpose of these phrases. 'War is war' is not an example of the law of identity either.

One of the purposes of a phrase such as 'I know . . .' is to contrast my own relation to my sensations with that of others. Other people have to use the evidence of what I say or do in order to claim anything about what I feel, and, to this extent, always run the risk of being wrong. In my own case, however, though not using any evidence, I cannot be wrong. Similarly, the examples of things which Moore claimed to know do not rest on grounds which are themselves more certain. My having two hands, for instance, is, in normal circumstances, as certain as anything that I could produce in evidence for it. This is why I am not in a position to take the sight of my hand as evidence for its existence (*OC* 250; and also cf. *OC* 245). For if I am now in doubt whether I have two hands, I need not believe my eyes either (*PI* II, page 221). But the fact that the things Moore claimed to know are not such as to be backed up by evidence—or doubted, or vulnerable to mistake—makes them, according to Wittgenstein, things which it is senseless to claim to know:

> But if what he believes is of such a kind that the grounds that he can give are no surer than his assertion, then he cannot say that he knows what he believes. (*OC* 243)

This point is an essential part of Wittgenstein's overall position. To reject it is to reject his view that any account of knowing that something is true is inseparable from an account of the relevant evidence. And it is one of the substantive points against which criticism of *On Certainty* has been directed. Such criticism depends on a contrasting view of meaning and truth—issues with which Unit 32 will specifically deal.

We saw in section 1 that a request for evidence in support of a claim to knowledge must stop somewhere if there is to be certainty on any matter, and that many philosophers, such as Descartes and Russell, have said that this stopping-place must be at the level of a proposition or set of propositions which is in some sense self-guaranteeing. Now Moore has not suggested that the things which he claims to know play any foundational role in a system of knowledge—merely that they are as good test cases as any for supporting the belief that there is an external world, and that it would be absurd to raise any doubt about them. Wittgenstein accepts that Moore has given examples of things which, in most circumstances, are indubitable, and, as we shall see in section 4, he also sees them as playing a foundational role in all judgement. But he denies that they are things which it makes any sense to claim to know. If, he says (*OC* 58), there is no such thing as doubt in the sorts of case which Moore presents, then, in effect, the expression 'I do not know' makes no sense. And from this it follows that 'I know' makes no sense either. It is quite clear here that Wittgenstein is not interested in either confirming or denying that Moore knows whatever he claims to know: he is concerned only with the question whether it *makes sense* to say one knows. At *OC* 10, for instance, he says that if I am attending on a sick person, neither the assertion that I know that this is a sick man lying here, nor the question whether I do know it or not, *makes sense*.

Wittgenstein's position in *On Certainty*, then, is an application to the question of knowledge of his views about sense and meaning that he developed in the *Philosophical Investigations*. Further on in the note at *OC* 10 he reiterates the point, familiar to you from the *Investigations* and from Units 14–22, that it is only in use that a proposition has sense. (Compare also *OC* 432–33.) There is a quite sustained discussion of this point, in relation to the sense of expressions used to make a claim to knowledge, at *OC* 347–51.

At *OC* 451 Wittgenstein says that his objection against Moore is that the meaning of 'That is a tree', said in isolation from a context in which it is clear why it is being said, is undetermined. The 'that' in 'That is a tree', or the 'here' in 'Here is one hand', is informative and secures an identification only once the context in which it is being used is understood. At *OC* 349 Wittgenstein gives examples of how the 'that' which I declare to be a tree could refer to different things. If I say, 'I know *that*'s a tree', for instance, I may be contrasting myself with someone who thinks it's a shrub. As Wittgenstein says in *OC* 622, each one of Moore's examples could be given a determining context—circumstances could be imagined in which they had a point. (He gives a rather fantastic illustration, in *OC* 264, of how one of Moore's examples could be made sense of.) But Moore has uttered the sentence 'I know that that's a tree' in no such determining context. As a result, it is difficult, as Wittgenstein puts it at *OC* 347, to 'focus on its meaning'.

Moore *has* used the expression in a determining context, however, hasn't he? He's used it in a philosophical context—that is, in a context in which there are reasons for claiming to know obvious things (*OC* 467). Wittgenstein, in fact, does recognize why Moore wants to insist that he knows that there's a tree before him. At *OC* 350, he agrees that one might insist on this in an attempt to establish that it is possible to speak of knowledge of things which are not true by necessity. But Moore's mere insistence that he *does* know doesn't meet the arguments put forward by the sceptic for insisting in turn that, wherever error is conceivable, claims to knowledge are ill-founded. Basing himself on the considerations raised in section 1, the sceptic can retort, 'You don't *know* anything'. (See *OC* 406–08.) So to use 'I know' in this context doesn't do anything to remove any doubts supposedly arising from these sorts of considerations.

However, there are several passages in which Wittgenstein displays the same doubts that most people seem to have about his own insistence that it is incorrect to use 'I know' in the sorts of cases used by Moore: in the remark at the end of *OC* 552, for instance, and at *OC* 464, where he says that his difficulty can be put by asking, 'Isn't it just that the remark that I know in these cases is *superfluous*, though true?' And at 397 he asks, 'Haven't I gone

[margin note:] sceptic will argue that whatever error is conceivable – claims to knowledge are ill founded.

[margin note:] 'I know superfluous'.

wrong and isn't Moore perfectly right?' That is, isn't Moore right to have insisted that he *knew* that the earth already existed for some time before my birth, and hasn't he, Wittgenstein, been making the elementary mistake of thinking that knowing something involves thinking about it?

His reply to himself on this last point is at the end of *OC 480*. It is a repetition of the point that to know something, even if one isn't thinking about it, involves the notion that what one knows is something which it is possible to doubt. But someone could restate the question behind Wittgenstein's doubts here in this way: 'If someone says "I know that that's a tree" although there is no possibility of doubt, then it might be unclear *what the person meant* by what he said, but we all know the *meaning of the sentence* he used. And what is meant by "the meaning of the sentence" here is what is determined by the structure of the sentence and the meanings of its parts (for example, its words). And what is meant by "the meaning of the words" is what is given in dictionaries. It's not clear that what Wittgenstein is going on about is what we understand by "meaning" at all!'

Any properly adequate answer to this objection would require a detailed account of Wittgenstein's view of the role of ostensive definition in meaning and of his idea of what is involved in following a rule for the correct use of any term. Drawing on your studies in the second half of A402, however, what sort of defence of Wittgenstein's position could you *briefly* give to this very reasonable objection? My own response will be very brief and quite possibly less adequate than yours. Please don't skip this exercise, though, as it's a chance to test your own understanding of this half of the course.

It is true that the meaning of a sentence or a word *in a language which we already understand* can be understood even though we don't understand what someone meant by his use of those words, or though the word or sentence isn't actually said by anyone at all (for example, when it's used as an example in an English grammar book). But this is only because we know the circumstances and situations in which we should understand what someone meant by using the word or sentence. Wittgenstein's emphasis on the rule-governed *use* of a word or expression was made largely to lessen the limitations of those accounts of meaning which rest, at some basic level, on the correlation of words or sentences (which at this level are just *sounds*) with non-linguistically identified objects or situations (which may be physical objects or ideas or sensations). For before a sound can be used *meaningfully*—i.e., be recognized as a word or group of words which can be used again in a relevantly similar way—there has to be some prior understanding of just which object or situation, or aspect of them, is being correlated with the sound. And this we understand by recognizing the use to which the utterance is being put in a particular situation. So Wittgenstein's account of meaning consists ultimately of a description of the ways in which people respond to and interact with each other and to their situations. At a more sophisticated level, a dictionary can be devised which traces both the correlations among different words in a language and the natural and conventional changes in use. There are many places in *On Certainty* (e.g. the end of *OC 10*) where Wittgenstein draws attention to the fact that we use the expression 'I know such and such' in situations in which we wish to remove a doubt that such and such might not be the case.

To repeat, then: Wittgenstein's criticism of Moore's saying that he *knows* certain sorts of things to be true depends essentially on his own account of meaning and truth. If we say to Wittgenstein that we agree that there may be no *point*, in most cases, in saying that we know the sorts of things which

[handwritten: I know is contain the sense of proposition relation]

Moore claimed to know, but that it nevertheless remains *true* that we do know, then he can retort that to be able to ask whether or not something is true, we first have to be satisfied that it has sense. We'll be taking this issue up again in section 3, when we look at Wittgenstein's remarks about knowing whether or not one is dreaming.

2.3 REVIEW AND CHALLENGE

I'm now going to discuss *OC* 90, as a means of quickly reviewing this section of the units. Please read through it and note down the point of Wittgenstein's analogy between knowing and seeing.

In the way in which I cannot say 'I saw it, but it was not there', I also cannot say 'I know it, but it is not true'. If I do know it, then I am justified in inferring that it is so. But acknowledging that this inference is possible can mislead us into thinking that 'I know' is the expression of my relation to some fact (the relation of knowing it), in the way in which 'I believe' can be said to express a relation between myself and what I believe. If we do think this, then, just as the proposition describing what I believe identifies my belief, and my belief is an item in my consciousness, so it would look as if whatever it is that I claim to be a fact is similarly an item of my consciousness. But we should then have to find some fact about which we are infallible before we could claim to know anything. I can be mistaken in thinking that I saw Tom, who I knew was in the room wearing a red shirt, but I cannot be mistaken in thinking that I had the sensation of seeing a red patch. Such things as this sensation of a red patch, it might be claimed, which is an item of consciousness (a datum of the senses), are the only objects of knowledge or perception. As you know, Russell did in fact claim that there were things having this status. But then, as we have seen in the case of Hume, there arises the question of the connection between, on the one hand, these ideas of sense and, on the other, the events or things which are in the 'outer world' and which are not items of consciousness from which light-waves project to the eye and into consciousness.

About this, Wittgenstein claims that such an approach involves working with a false picture or model of knowledge, at the basis of which is the idea that we can or should only speak of knowing what we cannot be wrong about, just as we can only speak of seeing what is there to be seen. And this picture can lead us in turn to search for things about which we are infallible, whether these are the sorts of things which might satisfy Descartes, or which Russell thought of as sense-data, or which Moore had enumerated.

But how does all this leave Wittgenstein with respect to the sceptical arguments? He agrees with Moore that Moore's examples are of the sorts of things which are indubitable. But the sceptical considerations attempt to show that there is room for doubt even in these sorts of cases. What account can Wittgenstein give of those things which he agrees one can meaningfully claim to know, which would satisfy the sceptic? Wittgenstein, as we have seen, stresses two interrelated requirements for the use of 'I know'. Firstly, the fact that it is possible to be wrong in thinking one knows shows that the claim is something about which one can be mistaken: i.e., a claim to knowledge does not need to be confined to cases where a person cannot be mistaken, but includes cases where he only thinks that he is not. Thus, it

[handwritten margin: (2— the interrelated requirement for I know) (1) I am not possible wrong]

must be the sort of claim which it makes sense to doubt or to suppose that one could be wrong about. Secondly, whether one is right or wrong in claiming to know is a matter which can be backed up by evidence which will tell one way or the other. In other words, saying 'I know' can be backed up by grounds showing how one knows, grounds which give evidence for the truth of that which one claims to know. Wittgenstein has to give some account, then, of what counts as an adequate or conclusive ground for a claim to knowledge.

At *OC* 15–16 he says that whether or not someone's claim to knowledge is right has to be established objectively. But when is something objectively certain? Wittgenstein raises this question at *OC* 194, and his reply is: 'when a mistake is not possible'. The sceptical arguments, however, emphasize the possibility of mistake, by pressing such questions as 'How do you know that you are not dreaming or hallucinating?' So it might seem that mistakes would need to be *logically* excluded (cf. *OC* 194)—that is, that what I claim to know would have to be derived from truths about which it is impossible to be wrong. At *OC* 59 Wittgenstein says that, although Moore was wrong to make the point about his examples by simply saying he knew them, the actual examples he chose revealed a *logical* insight. Wittgenstein's reply to the sceptic involves rejecting the idea that a mistake be *logically excluded* in the above sense, but it also rests upon his claim that the sort of propositions which Moore lists *play a logical role* in any system of knowledge or judgement. In section 4 we shall see what this logical role involves.

Our next job, however, is to see what Wittgenstein makes of the sceptical reasons for suggesting that we might be mistaken about those things which Moore listed: what he makes of the claims that there is room for doubt even in these cases and that we have to find cases in which doubt is logically excluded.

3 DOUBT

3.1 LIMITS TO WHAT CAN BE DOUBTED

Descartes said, you remember, that in order to examine the truth it is necessary once in one's life to doubt of all things, so far as this is possible. In section 1 I emphasized that Descartes required this not just as an academic exercise, but as a means of rationally assessing our most fundamental and significant beliefs about the world and any new beliefs presented to us by scientific development and change or through meeting different people. But if we take Descartes' sceptical programme seriously we seem to be led quickly to the conclusion that the scope of knowledge is very limited indeed. So we need to return to Descartes' programme of systematic doubt and ask, just *how far* is it possible to doubt of all things?

In the *Discourse* Descartes extends the possibility of doubt by means of three considerations. He writes:

> [Because] I wished to give myself entirely to the search after Truth, I thought that it was necessary for me to take an apparently opposite course, and to reject as absolutely false everything as to which I could imagine the least ground of doubt, in order to see if afterwards there remained anything in my belief that was entirely certain. Thus, because our senses sometimes deceive us, I wished to suppose that nothing is just as they cause us to imagine it to be; and because there are men who deceive themselves in their reasoning and fall into paralogisms, even concerning the simplest matters of geometry, and judging that I was as subject to error as was any other, I rejected as false all the reasons formerly accepted by me as demonstrations. And since all the same thoughts and conceptions which we have while awake may also come to us in sleep, without any of them being at that time true, I resolved to assume that everything that ever entered into my mind was no more true than the illusions of my dreams. (*Discourse*, IV)[1]

We can agree with Descartes that only that is certain which is indubitable, but if we also agree with his reasons for extending so widely the limits of what is dubitable, then it seems that next to nothing is certain. In this section, then, we'll look at these reasons for doubting in connection with Wittgenstein's question at *OC* 2 whether it makes sense, for Descartes, to doubt the sorts of things which he tries to doubt.

Wittgenstein's arguments against radical doubt turn again, as they did in the case of knowledge, on his view of when an expression of doubt *makes sense*. According to Wittgenstein, a claim to knowledge or certainty in relation to questions of doubt is correct if it is a claim about the sort of matter which it *makes sense to doubt* but which it is *reasonable* to say is, in the circumstances in which the claim is made, indubitable—if, that is, it is a claim which someone makes about himself or someone else to the effect that he is not, *in fact*, wrong or mistaken, or if it is made in the form: it is certain that there is in fact (rather than in principle) no doubt.

3.1.1 Making mistakes

We'll begin again with the question which Wittgenstein asks at *OC* 194: 'When is something objectively certain?' Someone is certain if he thinks that he hasn't made a mistake, but we could say that he is *objectively* certain if it is true that he hasn't, in fact, made any mistake. It seems plausible to suggest

[1] Cambridge ed., page 101 (Everyman ed., page 26).

- Objectively certain
mistake
logically
excluded

that the only cases in which we can be objectively certain, in this sense, are those in which a mistake is *logically* excluded. One way of understanding this point is to say that only those cases which somehow ensure their own validity can be candidates for certainty in any strict or rigorous sense. Descartes thought that he found such a case in his *cogito* argument.

Wittgenstein continues his point in the next note, at *OC* 195, but he does not take up in any direct way this question of a mistake's being logically excluded. Instead, he cites the example of being wrong in believing that I am sitting in my room. This, you remember, was also Descartes' example in *Meditation I*. If I am wrong about this, Wittgenstein says, I shall not be said to have *made a mistake*. There are several other remarks about making a mistake throughout *On Certainty*: I consider the ones at *OC* 74 and *OC* 574 to be centrally significant, and there is a sustained line of thought on the topic beginning at *OC* 630 to the end of the text. Please read through these sections now, and note your answer to the question why Wittgenstein wishes to say that the case at *OC* 195 is not a case of making a mistake.

Wittgenstein's ground for saying that believing I am sitting in my room when I am not is not a case of making a mistake is that there is an essential connection between mistakes and knowledge. *OC* 74 and 574 give some considerations in elucidation of this point. At *OC* 74 Wittgenstein suggests that a mistake has grounds, and grounds are to be contrasted with the cause of the mistake. The fact that a mistake has grounds means that the mistaken judgement can be fitted into what the person making it knows aright. I understand this as saying that a mistake involves a *judgement* which is made on the basis of the evidence of other judgements, about some of which, at least, I am right. For example, if I make a mistake about my direction, and believe that I am on the right road when I am not, then this belief can be fitted into what I do know, namely that I have the right map, that the map is accurate and that I should turn left off the main road. But my missing the correct turning may have a variety of *causes*: I may have been distracted by the magpie swooping across the road, for example. My mistaken belief, however, about being on the right road is *grounded* in the reasons I give for turning off at the point I do. Thus, to apply this argument to the case at *OC* 195, I may awake suddenly from a dream in which I dreamt that I was in my room, and so my dream can *cause* me momentarily to believe that I am there, but this belief cannot be fitted with the fact that I remember getting on the train and that I see that we have just passed Preston. I have made this example more complicated than you may think it need be, so as to avoid saying that my *dreaming* that I am in my room is itself a case of believing that I am. I shall go into this in 3.3.

At the end of *OC* 574 Wittgenstein again makes his point that a claim to knowledge can be tested. Thus, if someone says that I am mistaken in saying that I know that I am on the right road, we can test at the next signpost whether I am or not. Note that a minimum requirement for testing whether or not I am mistaken is that there should be agreement about what does decide the case, for if I am *deluded* about being in my room, as opposed to mistaken, then I may point to all sorts of things which I think support my belief, things which someone else might not acknowledge as evidence for my claim at all. Hence Wittgenstein's point (*OC* 156) that, in order to make a mistake, 'a man must already judge in conformity with mankind'. This is one of the many respects in which Wittgenstein's discussion about agreement in judgements at *PI* 242–243, which you studied in section 2 of Units 16–19, is relevant. I see Wittgenstein's point about agreement in judgements as pivotal to his whole discussion of meaning and certainty, and its application here brings out the importance of his remark at *PI* 241 that he is *not* saying that it is human agreement which decides what is true and what is false, but agreement *in the language used* to make true and false statements, agreement which, as he puts it, is 'agreement in form of life'. We'll take this question up again in sections 4 and 5.

A general point concerning the connection between mistakes and knowledge, on Wittgenstein's account, is that one can speak of being mistaken only about the sorts of things it makes sense to say one knows. I see this point as connecting with several remarks Wittgenstein makes in his notes about making a mistake, at *OC* 630 ff. and especially at *OC* 634. If 'the worst comes to the worst', i.e. even if all the evidence seems to point against me, and if I refuse to conceive that I may be mistaken (and if there doesn't seem any reason to suppose I have any psychological motive for being stubborn), then 'I shall make my proposition into a norm'. That is, I shall use my claim as a principle of judgement in terms of which I assess the evidence. So if I *could* not be mistaken about the matter, it is not, according to Wittgenstein's points about the use of 'I know', the sort of thing I should claim to know either. Moore's examples are examples of cases where it is impossible to be mistaken. However, there is no characteristic common to all his examples in virtue of which we can say that they *are* such examples (*OC* 674).

3.1.2 Universal doubt: Wittgenstein's argument against the sceptic

Descartes, however, speaks, not about making a mistake, but about the possibility of *doubting*. The notion of *doubt* is wider than that of a mistake. I make a mistake if I think that something is the case when it isn't. Although one reason I may have for doubting something is the suspicion that I may have made a mistake, this is not the only sort of reason.

We have just seen how Wittgenstein responds to the argument from the fact of error by saying that errors and mistakes can be corrected in the light of other things we know. So his reply to Descartes' emphasizing that errors often arise in judgements based on the evidence of the senses would be very similar to that of Hume. (See the *Enquiry*, Section 12, Part 1, discussed on pp. 9–10 above.) I said in section 1.2.1, however, that Hume's response to the argument from error ignored the import of Descartes' point: Descartes saw the possibility of error as a reason for questioning the general validity of sense perception as a source of knowledge. At first sight the same might be said about Wittgenstein's response to someone who claims to *doubt* such a thing as whether he has a body. At *OC* 257 Wittgenstein remarks, in response to this example, that he doesn't know of any way in which someone who claimed to doubt this could be convinced that he had, in fact, a body. This would be of no interest to Descartes, however, for he is interested in questioning the general adequacy of the grounds for convincing anyone of any empirical claim. In the terms in which I presented the issue in section 1.3, Descartes is bringing into question the very grounds on which people speak about their bodies at all.

Wittgenstein's argument, though, which does conflict with Descartes' is that Descartes' general questioning of empirical claims involves working with a false picture of doubt (cf. *OC* 249). I see the remark of *OC* 249 as connecting with Wittgenstein's remark in the *Philosophical Investigations*:

> It may easily look as if doubt merely *revealed* an existing gap in the foundations; so that secure understanding is only possible if we first doubt everything that

can be doubted, and then remove all these doubts. [But] the sign-post is in order—if, under normal circumstances, it fulfills its purpose. (*PI* 87)

This remark is made in the context of the discussion whether there can be a complete explanation of how a rule of language is to be applied (complete in the sense of obviating the possibility of misunderstanding the rule). This passage from the *Investigations* can be put alongside *OC* 392, where Wittgenstein says that the possibility of the language-game doesn't depend on everything being doubted that can be doubted. Part of what is involved here is that Descartes thinks he has to doubt everything that can be doubted in order to establish sure and indubitable foundations on which any other claim to knowledge can be based. Any claim to knowledge, or procedure of testing, can then be justified in an ultimate sense by displaying its place in the hierarchical system of knowledge. Wittgenstein, however, claims that a language-game such as that of testing and weighing the evidence for or against any claim to knowledge cannot be justified in this ultimate sense. For although Descartes is right in his observation that with *any* belief we can imagine circumstances in which it can be doubted, we cannot doubt everything at once. See *OC* 115: 'If you tried to doubt everything you would not get as far as doubting anything. The game of doubting itself presupposes certainty.'

An example is given at *OC* 114. One reason why Descartes would not get as far as doubting anything is that he would not be able to doubt the meaning of the words in which he expressed his doubt. *Now this is not a trivial point.* For it is part of the claim which is fundamental to the argument in *On Certainty*, namely that a doubt is not just a state of mind identified by some act of introspection, but something which can be expressed in terms of a *meaningful* sentence. This is *not* the point that, in order for any sentence to be meaningful in which, say, the word 'hand' or 'blue' occurs, there must *be* hands or blue things. The point is rather that, in order for any doubt to be raised about anything to do with hands, there have to be situations in which the word 'hand' can be used to some point. Or, to put this in a way which connects with *OC* 126, to be able to raise a doubt about any issue, I cannot at the same time doubt that my words have meaning. Thus I can ask, 'Is the colour of this object blue?' (if the object is seen in a dim light or if I'm not sure whether it's lilac) or, if my native language is not English, 'Is this colour called "blue"?', but I cannot ask this second question in order to doubt that my words have meaning. At *OC* 370 Wittgenstein says that the fact that I use the word 'hand', in any sentence in which I raise a doubt about my hand, for instance, shows that absence of doubt belongs to the essence of the language-game. If I ask, 'How do I know that I have put my fingers in the right position when playing this instrument?' then I am 'dragging out', or sustaining, the language-game concerning hands. But if I seriously claim to doubt that I have two hands and ask 'How do I know that I have two hands?' (when the circumstances are not exceptional), then I am doing away with *all* the linguistic interchange I can have about hands, *including doubting whether I have any.*

However, how does this argument work with a word such as 'unicorn', do you think? (Wittgenstein has a comment bearing on this at *OC* 476.)

If I seriously claim to doubt that there are any unicorns, then my doubt, far from doing away with all the linguistic interchange I can have about unicorns, involves a claim which is in fact true. There are no unicorns. But my doubt about whether there are unicorns does not amount to the question,

'Does the word "unicorn" have sense in *any* context?', which is the sort of question which the sceptic is raising about the word 'hand'; rather, it is to be understood as the question, 'Are there any unicorns to be found in the world, rather than in works of imaginative literature?' That is, the question does not attempt to undermine the use of the word 'unicorn' in *all* contexts where it is used to speak of a mythical animal with quite specific distinguishing features.

The issue, however, is far more complex with a word such as 'God'. We'll touch on this in the final section of these units.

We have now arrived at the point at which to state what I consider to be the core of Wittgenstein's arguments against the sceptic. *The sceptic cannot intelligibly doubt the things which he claims to doubt, without undermining the language-games in which the words he uses to express his doubt get their sense.* Wittgenstein's notion of a language-game is at the centre of this argument. It is a notion that was first discussed in this course in Units 14–15. In section 2.1 of those units you saw how Wittgenstein introduced it as part of his attack on the idea that a word has a meaning in virtue of standing for an object which it names. For instance, in relation to the question, 'What account can we give of the meaning of the word "five"?', he specifically attacked the view that we can say its meaning is introduced into the language as the name of an idea, in the mind of the speaker, which the speaker can correlate with instances of collections of five things in the world. (See the end of *PI* 1.) According to this view, unless we can perform this correlation, the sense of the word is *indeterminate*. That is, the meaning of the word cannot be explained, in a way which would obviate any misunderstanding, unless we can pick out the thing (either something in the world or an idea in the mind) which it is its role to name. If the sense of an expression *can* be determined with the necessary exactness, it must be possible for us to be acquainted with the object which it names, in such a way that there can be no doubt when a statement about that object is true. It is in the framework of this view that there might seem to be the requirement that an adequate test of any empirical proposition must be understandable as such *in logic* (see *OC* 110).

In contrast, Wittgenstein argues that we have no clear understanding of the notion of 'exact explanation' employed in this account (*PI* 88), and that we do not need one. For if we consider any example of how the word 'five' is given sense in its use in day-to-day discourse, no such theory of what it *means* is in question; there is only the question of the use to which it is put in the activity in *terms of which* it gets its sense. (See also *PI* 23.) The words in question are woven in as part of the activity, are used according to rules, much as the actions or movements in a game are performed in accordance with the rules constituting the game. Thus when at *OC* 82 Wittgenstein says that what counts as an adequate test of a statement belongs to logic, he goes on to say in explanation: 'It belongs to the description of a language-game.' When he speaks of logic in the context of a language-game (cf. also *OC* 375), he is not referring to a system of rules of formal inference, defined in some strict sense, but to rules governing the distinction between sense and nonsense. Wittgenstein does not, then, have any use, in a way which would interest the sceptic, for the distinction made by Moore between the *proof* of a statement and *conclusive evidence* for its truth. (See page 25 above.) The passages in *On Certainty* explicitly connecting these issues about doubt and knowledge with the issues about meaning and the determinateness of sense in the *Investigations* are at *OC* 25–29. We'll look at *OC* 26 in section 3.3.

Wittgenstein gives three examples of language-games at *OC* 563, 564 and 566: the language-game of calculation in mathematics at *OC* 563, the language-game involved in counting and collecting bricks at *OC* 564, and the language-game with colours at *OC* 566. What counts as an adequate justification of a claim to knowledge within any of these language-games will be a question of the sorts of things being done in each case. At *OC* 563 Wittgenstein says that the justification of a claim to knowledge in mathematics is a proof. Accordingly, what counts as a test of a conclusion in mathematics can be shown by a description of the language-game of calculation and proof in mathematics. Although I can prove a conclusion in mathematics, I cannot prove *in the same sense* that I've weighed something correctly. But this does not mean that I'm any less justified, on Wittgenstein's account, in saying that *I know* what so many bricks weigh, if I've checked my weighing apparatus and checked that I've not made a mistake. That is, I need no justification of the method of weighing and assessing weight itself.

We'll now look at these points in connection with Descartes' claim to doubt that he has a body.

— Taking doubt outside language-game.

3.2   DESCARTES' EXISTENCE

Descartes argues that he can doubt that he has a body, but not that he exists, so that the existence of his body is not essential to *his* existence. The consequences of Descartes' move have been far-reaching. The radical dualism involved in the claim that 'I' am something separate from my body entails that what I think, feel, and perceive can be understood independently of the actions and situations of my body. Throughout the second half of this course you have been studying how Wittgenstein persistently attempts to undermine this view. In *On Certainty* we go right back to one of its sources. Can Descartes intelligibly doubt that he has a body?

Descartes says that he doubts that he has a body on the general grounds that his beliefs about his body are all gained through sense experience, and that, in other circumstances, his senses have deceived him. But in what way does Descartes doubt *that* he has a body, as opposed to doubting things *about* his body, as a result of his sense experience? Descartes could ask the question of *OC* 24, 'What right have I not to doubt the existence of my body?' Wittgenstein's reply there is that anyone who asks such a question is overlooking the fact that a doubt about existence only works in a language-game.

At *OC* 24 Wittgenstein is talking about the claim to doubt that *my hands* exist, and his remark is, of course, directed at Moore's attempt to counter such a doubt by saying that he knows that he has two hands. This point applies also to the example of doubting the existence of one's body. But whereas we can imagine language-games in which doubt about one's hands has a place, there seem to me to be none in which there could be a genuine doubt about the existence of one's body. There are certainly many language-games about his body into which we can imagine Descartes entering. We know how he suffered from the cold, especially in Sweden. He must also have suffered other ailments and discussed his condition with his doctor, perhaps the condition of some specific part of his body. He must often have visited his tailor, and was probably measured for his dressing-gown. The things Descartes complains of, the questions his doctor asks of him, and the doubts the doctor may have about Descartes' condition certainly depend on the fact that Descartes has a body to be examined. And to this extent, we can go along with Descartes and say that for anything to be probable (e.g. a diagnosis of his condition), some things must be certain or beyond doubt (in this case that he has certain symptoms, and, more fundamentally, that he has a body). But the relation of this fact of Descartes' having a body to the possibility of the language-game is not the relation which is described by saying that the language-game couldn't go on if Descartes hadn't got a body. For it's not at all clear what saying this could mean. Rather, medicine, tailoring and so forth wouldn't be intelligible activities if there were any serious doubt whether anyone was there to be examined or dressed. (Cf. *Zettel* 364.) The questions the doctor raises about Descartes' condition, and the doubts he may have had that Descartes would survive his attack of pneumonia, depend on the fact that a multitude of propositions are exempt from doubt. (See *OC* 341.)

The argument about the status of the question, 'Do I have a body?', which is involved in Descartes' doubt, is to some extent parallel to the argument about the status of the question, 'Do other people have pains?', which you studied in detail in Units 20–22. The denial or doubt that other people have sensations implicitly involves using a term whose sense depends on the criteria used in asking or saying anything about what people feel.

A general point in continuation of Wittgenstein's remark at *OC* 24 that a doubt about existence only works in a language-game is the following. To say of anything that it exists (or to deny or question whether it does) is not always to say the same sort of thing in different cases. (As, for instance, to say of anything that it is red, *is* always to say that it—whatever it is—is of a certain colour.) For in order to understand any statement to the effect that something exists (or does not exist), we first have to know what sort of thing it is. I would not be saying the same thing about coelacanths, ghosts and the highest prime number if I claimed that they existed, and doubts about the existence of these things would be raised in terms peculiar to each of them. An enquiry into whether King Arthur existed would be a very different matter from raising the question whether there is a seven in the decimal expansion of π; the 'language-game' about supposed historical personages is different from that of questions in mathematics. But, to paraphrase a remark at *OC* 255, it is difficult if not impossible to imagine what would constitute a language-game involving doubt about one's body. Descartes' claim to doubt such a thing in *Meditation I* is not an example of the use of doubt in a language-game, for the claim is made as a philosophical doubt; the notion of being able to doubt *is taken from circumstances in which there are means, in principle, of resolving the doubt, and is applied to cases where reference to such means is ruled out.*

3.3 DESCARTES' DREAM

If Wittgenstein is right, as I think he is, in claiming that Descartes cannot intelligibly doubt everything which he believes on the evidence of sense experience and that it is not at all clear what would be involved in doubting that one has a body, then the route which Descartes takes in *Meditation II* towards establishing the, for him, essential distinction between his body and his thinking self is blocked. The method of doubt had been instrumental in creating the *illusion*, as Wittgenstein put it previously in the *Blue Book*, that we use the word 'I' 'to refer to something bodiless, which has its seat in our body. In fact *this* seems to be the real ego the one of which it was said, "Cogito, ergo sum!" (*BB*, page 69).

However, we have so far ignored Descartes' argument that he might be dreaming and so be wrong in thinking that he was sitting by the fire in his study. In *OC* 643–44 Wittgenstein uses a similar argument to come to the opposite conclusion. He argues that cases of awakening and realizing one has only been dreaming that such and such was happening do not undermine the right to say that one can't be wrong: 'For otherwise, wouldn't all assertion be discredited in this way?' (*OC* 644). But to this Descartes would simply answer, 'Yes, that is my point'.

Wittgenstein's answer to the argument from dreaming is at *OC* 383:

> The argument 'I may be dreaming' is senseless for this reason: if I am dreaming, this remark is being dreamed as well—and indeed it is also being dreamed that these words have any meaning.

The validity of this argument obviously turns on Wittgenstein's view of meaning, to which we alluded in section 3.1.2 (page 41). The argument is repeated and illustrated in the final note of *On Certainty* (*OC* 676). If I utter the words 'I am dreaming' or 'I am sitting in my study' while I am actually lying asleep, then I am neither right in the former case, nor mistaken in the latter, for I have *not asserted* anything. (Wittgenstein discusses this point more fully at *Z* 396 ff.)

A. J. Ayer has criticized Wittgenstein's remarks about dreaming in his paper 'Wittgenstein on Certainty' in the Royal Institute of Philosophy series (published under the title *Understanding Wittgenstein*).[1] You would undoubtedly profit from reading the whole paper—in fact much of what Ayer says, especially at the beginning, would form a means of revising some of the points which I have been discussing. Much of Ayer's criticism of Wittgenstein's arguments stems from the fact that he holds a different view of meaning from Wittgenstein's. (This applies to his criticism of Wittgenstein's view of the place of 'I know', as well as to his criticisms of Wittgenstein's views on dreaming.) Please now read from page 237 of Ayer's article, starting from the bottom paragraph, and note your answer to this question: what differences are there between an account Wittgenstein might give of the meaning, or lack of meaning, of 'I am dreaming' and one which Ayer might give?

On page 238 of his article, it seems to me, Ayer is assuming the view that an utterance in the form of an assertion is meaningful *if there are conditions under which it is true*. He writes:

> For the proposition 'I truly believe that "*p*"' to be true, it is necessary and sufficient that '*p*' be true and that I also believe it. Suppose that '*p*' is the proposition 'I am dreaming'. In the cases that Wittgenstein envisages, this is true *ex hypothesi*.

'I am dreaming' is a meaningful statement for Ayer in so far as it may be true (or false). On page 240 Ayer says that the argument 'I may be dreaming' is not senseless, for it is an argument which uses a statement which may be true. And at the bottom of page 238 he says that if we allow that I can correctly remember that I dreamt that I was dreaming or that it was raining, then the words in which I express this recollection *have the same meaning* as the words, 'I am dreaming' or 'It is raining', with which I formulated my thought in my dream. I think that one reason for claiming that these words, occurring in two different situations (while one was awake and while one was asleep), have the same meaning would be that it is the same thing in both cases which makes them true—namely, in this example,

[1] G. Vesey (ed.), *Understanding Wittgenstein*, Macmillan (set book).

the fact that one was dreaming. In Ayer's case, then, I think there is good reason for saying that he is assuming the view that the meaning of a proposition is given in terms of its truth-conditions.

When Wittgenstein writes at *OC* 676 that someone's uttering the words 'I am dreaming' whilst asleep is not *right*, he is claiming that the person sleeping has not made an assertion at all: what *he* said was neither true *nor* false (cf. Ayer, page 239). His argument for this at *OC* 676 is that only someone who is conscious can speak truly or falsely about his situation. On page 238 of his article, Ayer says that he sees no good reason for this view. *Given Ayer's own views of meaning*, no convincing reason could be given him, for he regards words in the form of an assertion—a 'proposition'—as having a truth-value in isolation from their *use* by any speaker. What Wittgenstein says, however, rests on his own view of meaning, namely that 'it is only in use that the proposition has a sense' (*OC* 10). Anyone unconscious of his situation would be unaware both of the grounds which validate his making any assertion, and of the point, or use, of the assertion in that situation. (Cf. the illustration on page 62 of Units 23–24.)

This is one instance of the fact that any serious criticism of Wittgenstein is a criticism of his view that items of language are meaningful in virtue of the uses to which they can be put in actual situations; it shows that one standpoint from which this criticism can be made is the view that a language can be regarded as meaningful in virtue of the conditions which make certain forms of words *true*. This debate will be the topic of Unit 32.

3.4 DOUBT AND THE TRUTHS OF REASON

It was emphasized at several points in Units 1–2 that Descartes saw in the method of reasoning used in logic and mathematics a standard against which to measure the reasoning used to substantiate all other claims to knowledge. At the end of Rule II of the *Regulae*, he writes:

> ...in our search for the direct road towards truth we should busy ourselves with no object about which we cannot attain a certitude given to that of the demonstration of mathematics.[1]

Truths established by the methods used in arithmetic, geometry and formal logic may seem to have a privileged place with regard to certainty, since they are arrived at by a *universal* method of proof which can *systematically* eliminate all possibility of error and which makes no reference to the situation of any particular person working through the proof. In these terms, the truths of reason may be said to be arrived at *objectively*.

In the first *Meditation*, however, Descartes brings even these truths of reason into doubt. He does so by bringing in what may seem to be a somewhat artificial device, the idea of a deceiving demon. This can be seen as a merely colourful way of claiming that we can never be sure that we haven't made a mistake in calculation. But it can also be a means of asking a more searching question: that is, as a way of enquiring into the very foundations of logical and mathematical necessity. What is it that determines the nature of logical or necessary truths or the truths of geometry and mathematics? Why are they so binding? Are they true merely in virtue of rules or conventions peculiar to human thought, or are they true independently of any method of inference and calculation which people happen to use?

[1] Cambridge ed., page 5.

In Units 1–2, page 59, where these issues were first raised, you saw that Hobbes was in radical disagreement with Descartes concerning the issues and claimed that the truths of reason were the products of human convention.

At *OC* 436 Wittgenstein asks the question: are many of our statements *incapable* of being false, so that even God is bound by our knowledge? From the context of this question, it is clear that Wittgenstein has in mind statements of empirical fact. When he asks the questions elsewhere, in *PI* II, xi (page 226) and *Z* 357, about mathematical truths and the truths of reason, he does not distinguish mathematical truths from truths about the interrelationship between colours, which latter might seem to be examples of *empirical* truths. At *Zettel* 357, for instance, he asks:

> We have a colour system as we have a number system. Do the systems reside in *our* nature or in the nature of things?

(This section was discussed in Units 16–19, page 50.)

In view of the fact that Wittgenstein puts logical and empirical truths together here, it is obvious that he doesn't think that mathematical or logical truths have any privileged position in epistemology. I have already mentioned that he does not agree with Moore that the method of proof used in formal inference provides a standard against which other methods of inference and verification fall short—though as yet I have not said much about how he substantiates this claim. How he does so, and how he runs together logical and certain empirical propositions, is the topic of my next section.

At the points in *On Certainty* where Wittgenstein considers the certainty of mathematical propositions he mentions them as examples alongside, and not in contrast to, empirical examples. And at *OC* 651 he says that mathematical certainty cannot be contrasted with the relative uncertainty of empirical propositions. His reason for saying this is that the actions involved in working out a mathematical calculation, such as writing and remembering, are no different from the things we do in coming to conclusions in other areas, in so far as both kinds of actions are endangered by forgetfulness, oversight and illusion. He does go on in the following section, however, to say that mathematical propositions are incontestable and incontrovertible: contesting them is just not an option, and they are not subject to being overturned by contrary evidence. In the latter respect at least, however, they are no different from empirical propositions such as 'I am called...'

These remarks at *OC* 650–58 are reminiscent of the passages from *PI* II, xi (page 225–27), in which Wittgenstein makes similar points. There he again denies the picture of mathematics as providing an ideal of the highest certainty, but he faces more directly than he does in *On Certainty* the objections which could be put to him. He introduces the question whether his view commits him to saying that mathematical truth is dependent on human beings' knowing it. His view, then, that certainty in mathematics is of no higher order than the certainty of some propositions that have the form of empirical propositions is connected with his stance in relation to the question of the foundations of logical necessity. A way of putting the same issue, which engages more obviously with Wittgenstein's treatment, is this: in making an inference in accordance with a logical law or rule of calculation, are we responsible to anything other than the law itself? That is, is there anything beyond a rule or formula which determines how that rule is to be applied?

The passages which offer an answer in *On Certainty* are at *OC* 212, *OC* 217 and *OC* 26. At *OC* 212, in answer to the question whether or not we may be deceived when trusting to the result of a calculation, he writes:

> Somewhere we must be finished with justification, and then there remains the proposition that *this* is how we calculate.

At *OC* 217 he says that someone who questioned *all* the results of our calculation would be either thought crazy or regarded as someone who didn't rely on calculation and so 'reacted differently'; but it is not obvious how the person could be said to be *in error*, for a mistake, as previously emphasized, arises out of facts which the person making the mistake could be said to know, and in this case the person is putting the whole process of calculation into question.

On page 234 of his article 'Wittgenstein on Certainty' Ayer draws a parallel, in relation to this point, between a judgement arrived at by calculation and a judgement about the age of the earth. With the fundamentalist we have *no way of proving him to be in error*, as he is not in agreement about what counts as evidence. As we shall see, this point plays an important role in Wittgenstein's positive account of belief and certainty.

In so far as Descartes is claiming that we can never be sure that we have not made a mistake in our calculation, this point goes some way to answering Descartes. But in so far as Descartes' introduction of the demon serves to question the basis of the truths established by reason and calculation, Wittgenstein's remark that all we can do in the last analysis is describe the practice of calculation, seems to give Descartes rather short shrift. At *OC* 650, however, Wittgenstein replies again to the question whether it is possible that, even after a calculation has been checked over and over again, an error may have slipped in. Here the implication is that we need a rule or method with which to detect error, and this point (together with *OC* 26) underlines the argument, discussed at length in the *Investigations*, that at some stage, to avoid regress, we just have to describe a rule in order to justify the results of an inference or calculation. We cannot justify, at every point, the results of the application of a rule by reference to a further rule.

Wittgenstein's position here with regard to the foundation of the truths of reason is a particular application of his general view, fundamental to his view of language and meaning, that a rule of grammar—or in this case, a rule of inference or calculation—can have no *justification* in the sense of being determined by anything beyond its use and actual application. These issues were discussed at length in Units 16–19, sections 2, 6 and 4, under the description of the 'arbitrariness of grammar'.

It is this view which invites the ascription to Wittgenstein of the belief that language and logic are matters of convention. (See, for example, the article by Dummett, in the collection of papers edited by Pitcher, which deals with Wittgenstein on mathematics, and the defence of Wittgenstein in the paper by Stroud in the same volume.)[1] In neither of the two passages which I mentioned earlier, *Z* 357 or *PI* II, xi, does Wittgenstein actually state his position unequivocally. He does rule out the possibility of appealing to the world in order to justify a rule of language, for that would be like appealing to the results of a calculation in order to justify the method of calculation: it can only be done where one has an independent method of establishing the

[1] 'Wittgenstein's Philosophy of Mathematics' and 'Wittgenstein and Logical Necessity', in *Wittgenstein: The Philosophical Investigations*, ed. G. Pitcher, Macmillan, 1968.

results. He emphasizes instead that language, calculation and inference are founded on human agreement (e.g. *PI* 242–43, *Z* 428 ff.). Wittgenstein's apparent equivocation in response to the place of human convention arises because he wants to distinguish his own position, that this agreement is an agreement *in* language and practice, from the view he does not hold, that it is the result of decision or is subject to choice. Such agreement in practice depends in turn on the fact that people find it natural to respond or react in certain ways to each other and to situations. So Wittgenstein suggests that the person of *OC* 217, who doesn't trust any calculation, *reacts* differently.

In answer to the objector's remark on page 226 of *PI* II, xi that mathematical truth is independent of human beings' knowing it, Wittgenstein says that a denial of this view—for instance of the form 'human beings believe that $2 \times 2 = 4$'—hardly makes sense; yet he doesn't simply affirm the claim either, for he also says that it makes no sense to talk of mathematical truths independently of their place in calculations or a system of calculation. And he adds that a calculation is not merely a system of formal rules: describing it would involve describing a human practice (at a simple level, for example, counting operations and their applications). But, he then asks, could the practice be wrong? This is Descartes' question, in the stronger sense, about the deceiving demon. Wittgenstein's answer is to ask another question: is a coronation wrong?

The move here from talking about the diverse techniques and practices involved in doing mathematics to talking about the practices involved in performing a ceremony, is a further indication that Wittgenstein does not discriminate, in a philosophical sense, between beliefs or truths of reason and beliefs involved in any other activity. By using the phrase 'a philosophical sense', here, I mean that he does not isolate any one method for arriving at truth, for use as a standard against which to contrast others.

Having arrived at this point, I shall use it as a basis on which to sum up the whole of this section on doubt. Wittgenstein says that a doubt of a philosophical sort—that is, one which systematically attempts to undermine the procedures or methods used to resolve doubts in order to establish foundations for knowledge which are logically indubitable—is a mere form of words without sense. For a doubt which involves the possibility of mistake or error only makes sense in situations where there are, in principle at least, means of resolution, and the nature of these means depends in any one case on the sort of thing which it is at issue. Wittgenstein's way of putting this is that a doubt only works in a language-game: for example, a doubt about the result of a procedure or method of calculation can only be assessed in terms of that procedure; similarly, a doubt about the age of a tree or forest can only be resolved, *if* it can be resolved, in terms of the methods used for assessing the age of trees; a doubt about royal lineage can be cleared up only be reference to facts about ancestry. If a philosopher argues that, in order to be sure of any fact in these contexts, we first have to guarantee the validity of the methods we use to arrive at the truth, or prove that we cannot be wrong in thinking that there are physical objects such as trees or that people existed in the past, then he is demanding that we justify the appropriate language-games and validate the practices in which they are embedded. To do *this*, however, involves establishing a proposition or set of propositions which can be seen to be true and indubitable in isolation from *any* language-game or *any* area of discourse and activity (other than a philosophical one). This contravenes Wittgenstein's central view that it is only in use that a proposition, or an assertion which can be either true or false, has any meaning, and that it is only in terms of the practice of calculating, describing, discovering or whatever that we can formulate beliefs about ourselves or the world.

In the next section I shall go into further detail about the positive, as opposed to the critical, aspects of Wittgenstein's position. And in section 5 I shall look at some of the implications of this view. For the view might seem to involve the idea that beliefs form different systems, none of which can, as a whole, be questioned or validated. But, it might be objected (with reference to the three examples mentioned in the previous paragraph): there are different systems of measurement and calculation, some of which produce more accurate results than others; there is disagreement amongst scientists about the methods used to establish the age of trees; and beliefs held by those involved in a coronation ceremony—for example, belief in the divine right of Kings or in the political value of a monarch—can be questioned or seen to be false.

At this point, as we turn from those remarks in *On Certainty* which can be read as critical of both the sceptical positions against which Moore was arguing and Moore's own claims, and as we explore Wittgenstein's own position more fully, I think it will be useful to review the picture of knowledge which Wittgenstein was rejecting.

In the *Discourse* Descartes makes much use of architectural metaphors in describing knowledge. Knowledge is thought of as an edifice which should be constructed on solid foundations. The foundations are the first principles established by *metaphysics*, upon which are laid the ground floor of *physics* and the further storeys of *mechanics, medicine* and finally *morals*. Since the beliefs which Descartes had received from his fellow men, in his education and through learned books, presented so many conflicting opinions, he saw his task as that of rebuilding his *own* house of knowledge. It is, then, a private house, an epistemology of the first person (though, of course, he presumes all other houses to be the same).

There are several assumptions involved in Descartes' architectural analogy which have been shared by most thinkers working in the subsequent tradition of Western philosophy. Firstly, it assumes that the body of knowledge is a *unified system* or structure in which all instances of knowledge are related to one another in a *hierarchy* as parts of the whole. Secondly, it assumes that the system is *based upon a set of truths*, namely the foundations from which the rest is built up and which must stand firm if the building is to be trustworthy. Thirdly, it assumes that these truths must, if knowledge is to be possible at all, be *specifiable independently of any particular enquiry*—that the foundations can be displayed as such without regard to the superstructure. And, finally, it assumes that there are some *general criteria* for identifying these basic truths.

A consequence of these assumptions, in the tradition of epistemology since Descartes and Locke, is that the concept of knowledge has become disengaged from the learning of skills and the *processes* of enquiry and has become attached to the concept of certainty alone. It has become attached, in particular, through the line from Hume to Russell, to a certainty provided by the, or *my*, senses.[1] In this section I shall look at the remarks of *On Certainty* which relate to the claim that knowledge has *foundations*, for example:

> One might almost say that these foundation-walls are carried by the whole house. (*OC* 248)

> ...it seems impossible to say in any *individual* case that such-and-such must be beyond doubt if there is to be a language-game... (*OC* 519)

I shall also discuss remarks which deal with the idea that knowledge forms a *system*, for example:

> Our empirical propositions do not form a homogeneous mass. (*OC* 213)

> When we first begin to believe anything, what we believe is not a single proposition, it is a whole system of propositions.

---

[1] See the article by Cavell listed in the bibliography, for his discussion of this point in the context of a discussion of *King Lear*.

> It is not single axioms that strike us as obvious, it is a system in which consequences and promises give one another *mutual* support. (*OC* 141–42)

Wittgenstein's main emphasis in the positive remarks of *On Certainty* is on the connection between, on the one hand, knowledge and belief and, on the other, the processes of enquiry and investigation and the activities which underlie certain beliefs.

4.1   THE FOUNDATIONS OF KNOWLEDGE AND MEANING

There is of course, a direct connection between the arguments in support of the idea that knowledge must have foundations, and the arguments in support of the idea than an account of meaning must say something about the basic elements upon which any discourse must be founded. Just as there must be, so it is supposed, some statements, or set of statements, which can be known to be true and which have not been inferred from any others, so there must be some basic set of statements whose meanings are not to be explained in terms of other statements: at some ultimate level, what we say must get its meaning from direct correlation with the world outside language. In acknowledgement of this requirement, the task of philosophy widens to become that of establishing the statements which form the indispensable support of everything we can know or believe *and* can meaningfully say. In the earlier part of this course you studied in some detail the different programmes suggested for analysing the constituents of understanding (Units 1–4) or of language (Units 5–13) into their basic elements, culminating in the view (Units 11–13) which explicitly identified the conditions verifying a proposition with the conditions giving it its meaning. From Unit 14 onwards, on the other hand, you have been studying various facets of Wittgenstein's criticisms of the view of meaning based on these assumptions. Thus, according to Units 14–15, 'These [later] ideas of Wittgenstein's involve a rejection of any view according to which there is some fundamental form of description of the world to which all other meaningful description is to be reduced' (page 32). In Units 16–19, there was explicit discussion of Wittgenstein's rejection of the idea that ostensive definition played the logically basic role that some philosophers had supposed, discussion which led in turn to the general criticism of Locke's view that 'there is an "agreement" between language and reality in so far as language "conforms" to reality, and that it conforms in so far as the things for which words stand, "ideas", are derived, directly or indirectly, from passively-received impressions' (page 50). And Units 20–22 consisted of a detailed presentation of Wittgenstein's criticism of the view that there are truths to which I have *in principle* privileged and private access: notably, truths which describe my immediate experience or sensations, which have been favourite candidates for truths that are epistemologically or logically basic. (See particularly Units 20–22, pp. 8–9.)

In those accounts of meaning in which ostensive definition has a primary role, meaning rests on some kind of knowledge. At *OC* 477 Wittgenstein states the claim of one persuaded by such an account: 'One must know that the objects whose names one teaches a child by ostensive definition exist.' I take his question at the end of this section to be rhetorical—the language-game does *not* rest on some kind of knowledge. Yet Wittgenstein does not deny that there are certain propositions which play a foundational role in any language-game. In fact, his interest in Moore's propositions lies in the fact that they play this role. At *OC* 136–37 Wittgenstein says that the propositions which Moore has enumerated as examples of known truths are in fact very significant. But this is not because anyone can know them to be true: rather, it is that they all have a similar role, a peculiar logical role in the system of our empirical propositions. This means, among other things, that they are propositions which are beyond question, which 'stand fast', as Wittgenstein puts it at several points, if a particular process of investigation, enquiry or testing can proceed. *OC* 341 makes a similar point: questions or doubts that we might raise about some matter depend on the fact that some propositions are exempt from doubt. Doubt itself rests only on what is beyond doubt (*OC* 519). Such statements, however, are of themselves ambiguous. Do they imply:

> (a) that some things are indubitable, and specifiable as such, independently of any particular enquiry or investigation?

or

> (b) that, in some particular investigation, some things are in fact not doubted?

On the second alternative, all empirical propositions are possible candidates for being doubted, given appropriate circumstances, but not all at once; for, whichever proposition is being doubted, some others must be beyond doubt, although in other circumstances one of these others might itself be subject to doubt.

At *OC* 232 there is a direct indication in favour of the second alternative, and there is also a brief argument for it in the continuation of *OC* 519. There is a certain ambiguity in this passage too, however. The expression 'any individual case' might be taken to be referring to any individual case of a language-game. I read the passage, though, as saying that *since a language-game consists in the recurrent procedures of the game in time*, it seems impossible to say of *any particular proposition* that it must be beyond doubt. In other words, the circumstances in which we can ask questions or make statements about an object or situation can differ, so that what is beyond doubt in one set of circumstances may not be so in another.

This notion that a language-game takes place through time characterizes one of the major differences between Wittgenstein's later view of language and meaning and his earlier. You will remember that in Units 14–15 Stuart Brown made the point that the discussion of language-games in the early part of the *Investigations* was introduced in *contrast* to a view, which Wittgenstein attributed to Augustine, that a language is to be thought of as constituted primarily of words or expressions which are applied to *pre-linguistically* identified ideas—as though we already have a language in our head, for which we then learn the particular English, German, etc. words. Whether or not Augustine did hold this view is, I understand, a moot point,[1] but certainly Locke (in some passages), Hume, and Russell (at certain times) all did so. The point I wish to emphasize here is that such a picture of language is essentially *static*. Language, thought of either as essentially a collection of names for ideas or as a body of propositions, is laid up against the world in such a way that its constituents get their sense by being hooked onto the pre-linguistically individuated elements, in a once-and-for-all way, *before* going on to be used to say something. In the simplest version of this view, a word is the name of a thing or an idea. As you will remember from your study of Russell in Units 5–6, this view of meaning can be combined with a certain epistemology: one has first to know that the thing named by a

—*Tractatus*

---

[1] See the article by Kenny in *Understanding Wittgenstein*.

word exists in order to ensure that the word is meaningful. (See again *OC* 477.)

Throughout the *Investigations* Wittgenstein questioned whether this process of hooking-on was possible *as a foundation*. How, if this view was correct, did we hook the right word onto the right thing? (Which *name* picked out which *object*?) It had been thought that we secured the correct connection by the process of giving an ostensive definition. Wittgenstein, as you have seen, did not deny that ostensive definition plays an extremely important part in language-learning and that many words can only be learnt in this way. But he questioned whether the process is as straightforward as it seems. *Having* a sophisticated language, we can see nothing problematical concerning what certain words or expressions pick out, and we can overlook the fact that, *before* the words 'blue' or 'cow', say, can be learnt ostensively, the person learning them has to recognize just which feature of the situation—viz., the colour or the animal—is being referred to (Cf. *OC* 545–48. As Wittgenstein puts it, what the child knows is not something simple.) By contrast, Wittgenstein emphasized two points. Firstly, the activities which we enter into, in using language, are extremely diverse. Picking out something, and then saying something about it, is only one possibility; asking questions, giving orders, expressing our feelings or condition, giving encouragement, are just some of the others. But secondly—and this is of particular relevance to the idea that language has an essentially temporal characteristic—the act of pointing out the object or situation referred to by a word is not sufficient, *of itself*, to secure the required connection. For the question remains, how is this act connected with the subsequent use of the expression? How, in other words, is the definition to be followed? The mere act of pointing out does not ensure that the word is used in the right way on subsequent occasions. To use it in the right way is to use it according to a *rule*. And to use it in the right way is to use it in the *same* way as it was used before and in the same way as other people use it.

It is in this connection that we can read *OC* 306. In reply to the question, 'Do you know what the word "hand" means?', Wittgenstein urges us not to reply, 'I know what it means now for me'. Someone might say this if he were impressed by the idea that the only things he can be sure of are those things he is, at that moment, experiencing; so the word 'hand' would name such a thing. But then, how would he know that he has used that word about the same sort of thing on another occasion? For saying that the only things I can be sure of are those things which I am experiencing now—and that such and such a word means what I am experiencing now—undermines any possibility of being sure that I use the word on some other occasion to mean the same by it as I do now. Compare the remarks at *OC* 455. I think the reason why the words 'and objects' have been put into scare quotes in the English translation of this passage is to stress that the objects in question are not individuated in the sense presupposed by the account Wittgenstein is opposing.

In contrast, Wittgenstein emphasizes that an ostensive definition is only useful if the word is interwoven with an activity, so that just what is indicated by the word is apparent from the point and circumstances of the activity. And the interweaving of sounds into an activity is a language-game. In terms of the example of *OC* 306, then, to know what the word 'hand' means is to be able to use the expression by, for example, understanding what is required when someone says 'Shake hands', or 'Wash your hands', or even when someone asks for an object to be handed to him. (Even when the word is used metaphorically, as in 'to win hands down' the context of its use must be understood even though the original activity in which it had a literal use need not be known.) On nearly all occasions on which people speak about, or use, their or other people's hands, the proposition 'I have two hands' must be beyond doubt, but it cannot be required *always* to play this role. For there are those extreme circumstances in which the question whether someone has in fact got two hands can arise. Wittgenstein thinks, as we have seen, that it is wrong to conclude that being able to conceive of such circumstances is sufficient reason for casting doubt, in general, on the existence of his hands. It shows that the proposition has to be rejected as an example of a proposition which is *always* beyond doubt. Yet we are *not* to conclude from this that we can therefore be certain of nothing. For 'as a rule some empirical judgement or other must be beyond doubt' (*OC* 519).

We can read Wittgenstein's use of the metaphor of the house of knowledge at *OC* 248 as an inversion of Descartes' position. It isn't that the foundations have to be established, or assumed, before the results of any enquiry can be credited, but that no enquiry is intelligible if some things are not beyond question. Descartes had thought that at the foundation of all our knowledge lay propositions which we could *see*, clearly and distinctly, to be true. Wittgenstein, by contrast, writes:

> Giving grounds, however, justifying the evidence, comes to an end;—but the end is not certain propositions' striking us immediately as true, i.e. it is not a kind of *seeing* on our part; it is our *acting*, which lies at the bottom of the language-game. (*OC* 204)

4.2   KNOWLEDGE AND ACTION

At *OC* 341 Wittgenstein says that the propositions which must be exempt from doubt in any enquiry are like the hinges on which those enquiries turn. And at *OC* 343 he raises the question whether we just have to *assume* that these hinges must stay put if we want the door to turn. I think it would be wrong to think of the propositions (the hinges) resting at the fulcrum of any activity as assumptions which we just haven't time, chance, inclination or ability to investigate. At *OC* 411 Wittgenstein remarks that it sounds strange to say that we *assume* such a thing as that the earth has existed for many years past. It is something which 'forms the basis of action, and therefore, naturally, of thought'. (Compare *OC* 148.) Giving grounds in support of a belief comes to an end, but 'at the foundation of well-founded belief lies belief that is not founded' (*OC* 253). However, 'the end is not an unfounded presupposition: it is an ungrounded *way of acting*' (*OC* 110).

At *OC* 471 Wittgenstein says that it is so difficult to find the beginning, though he then modifies this to say that it is difficult not to want to go further back than the beginning. On Wittgenstein's account, the beginning is what we find it natural to do. Compare: 'In the beginning was the *deed*'—the quotation from Goethe at *OC* 402. (Wittgenstein precedes his comment at 471 with the remark that there is a big gap in his thinking. I have to admit that I cannot suggest what he may have had in mind. Others more critical of the text than myself would possibly speak of a gap between being able to *do* something and being able to *say* something about what is done, emphasizing that a language is a symbol system, the application of which has to be accounted for. But I think this overlooks the fact that Wittgenstein puts more emphasis on the view that language is a sophisticated extension of gesture and exclamation.)

You may remember that Wittgenstein is not the first to have emphasized the facts of action in response to the preoccupations of the philosophical sceptic. Locke wrote in the *Essay*, for instance, that 'no man requires greater certainty to govern his actions by than what is as certain as his actions themselves' (IV. xi. 8). This is a remark which would not be out of place in the text of *On Certainty*. And from your reading of Hume's *Enquiry* in section 1, you may remember that Hume also thought that sceptical arguments lose their compulsion in face of the fact that they do not have the slightest effect on what people actually do: 'The great subverter of *Pyrrhonism* or the excessive principles of scepticism is action, and employment, and the occupations of common life' (*Enquiry*, Sect. xii, Part 2). But there is a difference between the role Wittgenstein gives to action *vis-à-vis* the sceptical arguments and that given it by Locke or Hume. Wittgenstein's emphasis on action is an *essential* part of his account of meaning. Hume, on the other hand, thinks that the facts of action and the conduct of our daily life refute the sceptical arguments only in the sense that they are incompatible with them and that the way we act and live, unlike the sceptical arguments, cannot be disregarded. Wittgenstein wants to counter the sceptical arguments by refusing to acknowledge that the things the sceptic claims to doubt can *intelligibly* be doubted. It is an essential feature of this picture that discourse involving doubt or certainty is *founded* on action. So reference to what people actually *do* is an essential part of the argument against the sceptic. (Cf. Z 416 and 419: in learning to speak about such things as tables and chairs, the child doesn't first have to learn that they exist, or assume that they do. 'There isn't any question of certainty yet in their language-game. Remember, they are learning to *do* something... Any explanation has its foundation in training.')

In this sense, knowledge requires that the instinctive or *animal* part of man, as opposed to the ratiocinative part, be given a proper place. (See *OC* 475.) This point is illustrated at *OC* 478, 538 and 540. In order to react to a mouse, the cat need not first *know* that a mouse exists (*OC* 478); he doesn't first have to establish it as true. Rather, any sense there *might* be in saying of a cat that it knows such and such about a mouse depends on the fact that the cat is able to react to the mouse in the way it does. Similarly, a baby doesn't *know* that there is milk. It acts instinctively and reacts in a certain way; 'in so reacting it doesn't so far know anything' (*OC* 538). A dog can be trained to respond to a sound which we identify as someone's name. But that is not enough to enable us to say that the dog knows what the person is called (cf. *OC* 540). In this sense, when the sceptic asks for a justification of a language-game, in order that the methods of proof and testing used within it can be validated, he can be given nothing more than a description of the facts, which he already knows perfectly well, on which the language-game rests. The bases of our practices are not called into question: they are there—'like our life' (*OC* 559).

4.3 RULE AND PROPOSITION

There is a further aspect of the point that it is misleading or inaccurate to think of the propositions lying at the foundation of any discourse as assumptions, as though the possibility that we might be mistaken about them were left open; Wittgenstein says that these propositions play a *logical* role in discourse. The propositions which Moore claimed to know, without any doubt, to be true interest Wittgenstein precisely because they are examples of propositions which, although *empirical* (they make claims about what is the case in the world), play a logical role in the sense that they draw the limits to what it *makes sense* to say or ask. I remarked earlier that Wittgenstein in his later writings uses the notion of logic in a wider sense than do those who confine it to the purely formal or syntactical rules governing propositions; he uses it to include those propositions, such as 'blue is darker than white' (*Z* 347), which are rules for the content of what can be said. Thus what interests Wittgenstein about the examples Moore gives is that no doubt concerning certain empirical propositions can exist if the making of judgements, correct or incorrect, is to be possible at all. 'Not everything that has the form of an empirical proposition *is* one.' (The two foregoing sentences derive largely from *OC* 308. Compare also *OC* 149–53.) The propositions in question are neither assumptions, nor *presuppositions*. (A proposition such as 'The earth has existed since a long time before my birth' only gets its *sense* from the things we can do and say about objects and the passing of time.) Nor are they *hypotheses*, i.e. propositions which can be confirmed or disconfirmed by later experience (*OC* 59–60). They are, less misleadingly, seen as *rules* of grammar or logic (*OC* 309, 494).

I regard sections 401 and 402 of *On Certainty* as containing the core of the position Wittgenstein works towards in that text:

> 401. I want to say: propositions of the form of empirical proposition, and not only propositions of logic, form the foundation of all operating with thought (with language).—This observation is not of the form 'I know...'. 'I know...' states what *I* know, and that is not of logical interest.

> 402. In this remark the expression 'propositions of the form of empirical propositions' is itself thoroughly bad; the statements in question are statements about material objects. And they do not serve as foundations in the same way as hypotheses which, if they turn out to be false, are replaced by others.
>   ...und schreib getrost
>   'Im Anfang war die Tat'.

We can see from *OC* 400, as well as from *OC* 402, that Wittgenstein was dissatisfied with the way he himself wanted to characterize the propositions which Moore had individuated by saying that he knew them. The expression 'propositions of the form of empirical propositions' is reminiscent of the *Tractatus* where, in the context of an account of the *general form* of a proposition, Wittgenstein gave a detailed account of the distinction between propositions which state what is or is not the case in the world, and propositions of logic, which say nothing. According to Wittgenstein's later view, however (cf. Units 14–15, sections 3.4), there is no such general account to be given, and the distinction between logical and empirical propositions does not always have a clear application. In the *Tractatus* a proposition was the primary unit of meaning in a language, and the meaning of a proposition could be determined by reference to conditions under which it was true or false. In this sense, a proposition was a sort of hypothesis held out to reality. The propositions enumerated by Moore, however, were not hypotheses. (Compare *OC* 52.) The proposition, 'At this distance from the sun there is a planet' can be put forward as a hypothesis to explain the occurrence of some phenomenon, and may later be confirmed or disconfirmed. But 'Here is a hand' is not put forward to *explain* the visual or tactile sensations I may be having. It does not say something which would be confirmed or disconfirmed by later experience.'

Wittgenstein says at *OC* 402 that the statements in question are statements about material objects. Moore's statements had been about material objects and he had used some of them to prove that material objects existed. In doing so he had been responding to those philosophers, such as the idealists and Russell, who had been impressed by the sorts of argument which we cited from Hume's *Enquiry* in section 1.2. Wittgenstein's reply to those arguments in *OC* 401–02, arising out of his interest in the way Moore dealt with the matter, is a continuation of his argument in *OC* 35–37. At *OC* 36 he gives some indication of how the propositions in question can be seen as rules of logic. Moore held up his hand, saying, 'Here is a hand', in order to claim, 'This is a physical object'. Wittgenstein remarks that the expression 'A is a physical object' is an instruction about the use of words. To say of something A that it is a physical object is to say what sort of thing it is, which is, in turn, to say what sorts of things can sensibly be said with the term 'A' or about the thing. 'There are physical objects' has the form of a statement about what there is, and so is a statement which can be denied or questioned, which is what the sceptic does, or affirmed and defended, which is what Moore did. Wittgenstein denies that it is an example of a sentence which can be used to make a statement of empirical fact. He says that 'physical object' is a logical concept, adding, in parenthesis: 'like colour'. He discusses an example in relation to colour at *Z* 331:

> One is tempted to justify rules of grammar by sentences like 'But there really are four primary colours'. And saying that the rules of grammar are arbitrary is directed against the possibility of this justification, which is constructed on the model of justifying a sentence by pointing to what verifies it.

Moore had wanted to justify the way we speak about objects like hands and our bodies by saying, 'There really are physical objects: I can prove it by holding up my two hands as examples'. Wittgenstein, in contrast, is claiming that 'A hand is a physical object' is not something which can be affirmed or denied: rather, it is a rule, or an instruction, about the grammar of the term 'hand'.

Wittgenstein's use of the notion of the *grammar* of a word and of a *rule* of grammar was discussed in some detail in Units 16–19, especially in section 2. You may already have thought to yourself, in reading those units, that these aspects of Wittgenstein's use of the notion of logical grammar are continuous with the thesis of *logical form* in the *Tractatus*: viz., that an object cannot be thought of independently of its being a constituent of certain states of affairs and that what sort of a thing an object is depends on its internal properties, which are shown by the states of affairs into which it can enter (*T* 2.0212–2.01231). Now, although what Wittgenstein means by 'object' in the *Tractatus* is radically different from what he means when he uses the term in the later works, there is a parallel between what he says in the later and in the earlier works. If we think of 'object' in the mundane sense as a loose term for a hand or a book, for example, then understanding the meaning of the word 'hand' or 'book' cannot be a matter of understanding what objects the words name, *independently* of understanding what sorts of things can be done with those objects or of understanding in what sort of situations they can play a part. So learning that hands and chairs are physical objects consists in nothing over and above learning how to speak informatively using the words 'hand' or 'book'. It is not the case that we first have to be sure that hands are not like after-images, which disappear or cease to exist when we are not paying attention to them, *before* we can go on to speak about them (*OC* 153). In answer to the question in *OC* 479, we can say that the *knowledge that there are physical objects* comes neither very early (i.e. *before* we can speak about things we are not directly experiencing) nor very late (i.e. after we have learnt to do so, or as an inference from how things appear). The *Tractatus* thesis of saying and showing, then, still plays a part in

Wittgenstein's later views, to the extent that the sorts of proposition which play a logical role—propositions such as those listed by Moore—cannot be affirmed or denied, or argued for or refuted; their unquestionable status is shown in what we know, say and do. 'Children do not learn *that books exist* ... they learn to fetch books' and read and talk about them (*OC* 476). Even though the proposition 'The table is there even when no-one is there to see it' has the form of an empirical proposition, it plays the role of a *logical* proposition, in the sense that it is something against which we may judge the *sense or nonsense* of anything said about tables. Macbeth felt quite secure that Birnam Wood would never come to Dunsinane; he felt that he had *logic* on his side. It is inconceivable for a wood to move. And in one sense, the sense that interests us here, Macbeth was right. Woods are not like clouds; they do not move around. Put in this way, this fact is a fact about woods. But we could also say that the grammar of the term 'wood' is different from the grammar of the term 'cloud', meaning that what it *makes sense* to say about the one is different from what it makes sense to say about the other. But if it doesn't make sense to say it, it doesn't make sense to think it either. In this way, *language*, *thought* and *reality* are essentially connected.

However, says Wittgenstein (*OC* 318), there is no sharp boundary between propositions which play such a logical role and very similar propositions such as, for instance (*OC* 237), 'An hour ago this table did not exist' (meaning, possibly, that it has only just been made), which is an empirical proposition and could be false. The former is a proposition which *characterizes* a method of judgement and enquiry, whilst the latter is a proposition which could occur in the use of such a method of judgement. It may be helpful to think of this distinction in terms of a more restricted example, say of playing a game like football. We can learn the rules of football (and so learn what a game such as football *is*) by playing it. We can distinguish between rules which describe what a game of football *is*, and descriptions of certain manoeuvres within the game which cannot be understood unless we have, independently, some understanding of the rules and the point of the game. The rules can be modified or altered without the game's ceasing to be a game of football, but there are some rules, the transgressing of which would radically alter the nature of the game, to the extent of making it into a different game, say rugby.

But there are two things to notice here. Firstly, unless we explicitly insist on a strict code of practice, there are no criteria according to which we *must* say that a change in the rules has changed the game into a different one. Secondly, the rules which, at any one time, are constitutive or descriptive of what the game is, cannot be brought into question *whilst the game is in play*, at risk of undermining the game. So within the context of the example of a game in the literal sense, such as football, there are rules governing the *language*-game involving the terms 'goal' or 'penalty'.

In the terms of this example of a game of football, then, the propositions describing the rules which are constitutive of the activity are, *at any one stage in the history of the game*, held fast, although the game can still alter through time. (The metaphor of the river and the river-bed in *OC* 96–97 might be read in application to this example.)

However, we must be very careful not to put too much emphasis on this example. A game like football is a conventional, quite well-defined activity, in which it is relatively easy to conceive of changing the rules. The rules governing the activity are the rules governing the correct use of terms describing the activity. And so, in the words of *OC* 138, the rules can be seen as part of *the determination of such concepts* as 'goal' and 'penalty'. But, at *OC*

138, the same point is made in connection with our earlier example: the proposition that the earth has existed over a great period. The concepts in the determination of which this proposition would play a role might either be very general ones, like 'history' or 'geology', or more specific ones, like 'carbon dating'. The proposition would here play an essential role in characterizing a method of establishing the age of something. And a method of scientific enquiry is very different from a method of playing a game. This is not only because the boundaries of the activity are far less clear, but also because it is *not open to us* to choose or alter the rules governing our methods, even though these methods *do* change (*OC* 256). In this example, it could be said that the world dictates to us, in a way in which it doesn't in the example of a game (though, even in a game, the rules which we *can* choose depend on very general facts about the nature of men and the world).

In this same connection, we must, I think, treat with caution Wittgenstein's saying (see *OC* 49 and *OC* 5) that we can *decide* when a method of calculation is 'fixed' or choose what counts as the determinant for a proposition. For even when the correct procedure of calculating with numbers is fixed for me, this fixing has *not* been decided by me, or by anyone else, with some practical purpose in mind. Examples of working out a calculation for a practical purpose might be drawing up the accounts of a business, or making a blue-print for an aeroplane: in these cases it is in no way up to us to *decide* what would be an appropriate calculation to employ, or to *decide* that the results we arrive at by using some method are the right ones. Wittgenstein cannot allow this, given all that he has said about the dependence of processes of coming to a decision, or of making judgements, on some things' being beyond deliberation. At *OC* 361 and 362 he rejects the idea that we take certain truths on the trust of an authority (such as, in Descartes' case, the authority of God), on the grounds that this would make knowledge rest on a decision: namely, the decision to recognize such an authority. Even if, as he says at *OC* 368, someone says that he will recognize no experience as proving the opposite of a proposition he regards as true, it is possible that what he *finds himself* doing will militate against such a decision. If we take the remark of *OC* 49 in its context, we see that it is part of Wittgenstein's insistence that there is nothing over and above the rule, and its application in practice, that justifies our proceeding, when calculating or whatever, according to such rules. Or, as he also puts the point, there is *no transcendent certainty*.

4.4 KNOWLEDGE AND INDUCTIVE EVIDENCE

In section 1 we saw that the sceptical arguments seem to require us to justify the way we arrive at any truth that goes beyond the present testimony of our senses, if any claim to knowledge is to be genuine. There seems to be a gap between the evidence, given in terms of what we hear or see, on which we base a judgement, and the judgement itself. This gap can only be convincingly closed, it would seem, by some process of inference. If the truth of the conclusion is to be reliably connected to the truth of the evidence, the connection must be made by one of two methods of inference: inductive or deductive. But, as Hume points out, matters of fact are not ascertained by demonstrative proof, as are the truths arrived at in geometry or algebra. For 'the contrary of every matter of fact is still possible, because it can never imply a contradiction, and is conceived by the mind with the same facility and distinctness, as if ever so conformable to reality'. We have seen how Wittgenstein also argues against this demand for a deductive standard for all knowledge. But Wittgenstein also critizes the assumption that, in many of the cases which interest the sceptic, there is *any* move from evidence to conclusion and so, *a fortiori*, any need for inference at all. Wittgenstein's use of the concept of a *criterion* cuts across this inferential gap. You were introduced to this notion in the Appendix to Units 11–13, though it has since then been only occasionally discussed in the course. If it is a coherent notion, as Wittgenstein uses it, then it is a powerful tool with which to break the traditionally exclusive dichotomy between the deductive and the inductive modes of inference, a dichotomy which has restricted many accounts of knowledge.

If I say, for example, that I know that someone is in pain, because of the way in which he is behaving, then I am saying *neither* that his behaviour entails, in a strictly deductive sense, that he is in pain (for I could be wrong in my judgement; he could be acting), *nor* that I infer that he is, on the inductive grounds that it has been my experience in the past that such behaviour goes with feeling a sensation of pain (for how would I know which sensation it 'goes with', or even that the behaviour goes with a *sensation*, except from my own case?) You will now have become aware, from Units 20–22, of the arguments which Wittgenstein believes weigh conclusively against the view that the word 'pain' gets its meaning, in the first instance, from naming something identified by my own introspective recognition. In fact, I don't infer at all from the other person's behaviour *to* something else which can be directly identified only in this way. His behaviour provides a criterion for the correct use of the word 'pain', but it does not ensure that I have made a correct judgement in using it. Similarly, I don't infer, in the great majority of cases, from my sensations to the fact that there is some object causing them. In the final unit of this course there will be a study of Wittgenstein's use of the notion of a criterion in relation to a more general account of meaning and truth.

But what about those cases in which I do infer from a proposition about something which I am now seeing, to the truth of some other proposition? Hume, you remember, said that we go beyond the evidence of our senses—say, from a letter we are at present reading, to the fact that the friend who sent the letter must now be in France—on the basis of our past experience: in this case, from experiences that arrivals of letters are caused by their being sent by their writers. We make an inference on the basis of a knowledge of which effects follow from which causes. But what is the basis of such knowledge?

There are several sections in *On Certainty* which have relevance to the issue as presented by Hume. But before looking at these, I should like to draw your attention to the fact that sections 472 ff. in the *Philosophical Investigations* also deal with the question. At *PI* 486, for instance, Wittgenstein, having first stated his position that there is no need for inference in certain cases, then goes on to speak of cases in which some question of inference is in place:

> Does it *follow* from the sense-impressions which I get that there is a chair over there?—How can a *proposition* follow from sense-impressions? Well, does it follow from the propositions which describe the sense-impressions? No.—But don't I infer that a chair is there from impressions, from sense-data?—I make no inference!—and yet I sometimes do. I see a photograph for example, and say 'There must have been a chair over there' or again 'From what I can see here I infer that there is a chair over there.' That is an inference; but not one belonging to logic. An inference is a transition to an assertion; and so also to the behaviour that corresponds to the assertion. 'I draw the consequences' not only in words, but also in action.

A passage which may help fill out the remark at the end of this section is the remark at *PI* 473:

> The belief that fire will burn me is of the same kind as the fear that it will burn me.

Here, the *action* which I perform in consequence of my realization that fire is hot is as much the expression of my belief that I shall get burnt as it is a consequence of my fear. But, as Wittgenstein says in the preceding section, such a fear or belief is based only on my experience in the past.

So what, you may now ask, is the difference between Wittgenstein's account and Hume's? From *PI* 472, at least, it looks as though Wittgenstein is saying that the belief in the uniformity of nature, the belief that the future will resemble the past in relevant respects, is based on nothing more than our experience of what has actually happened in the past, and that it is a belief revealed in terms of what we actually do. Compare these passages from Hume's *Enquiry*:

> It is certain that the most ignorant and stupid peasants—nay infants, nay even brute beasts—improve by experience, and learn the qualities of natural objects, by observing the effects which result from them. When a child has felt the sensation of pain from touching the flame of a candle, he will be careful not to put his hand near any candle; but will expect a similar effect from a cause which is similar in its sensible qualities and appearance . . . [but] it is not reasoning which engages us to suppose the past resembling the future, and to expect similar effects from causes which are, to appearances, similar. (*Enquiry*, Section 4, Part 2)

> All belief of matter of fact or real existence is derived merely from some object, present to the memory or senses, and a customary conjunction between that and some other object. Or in other words; having found, in many instances, that any two kinds of objects—flame and heat, snow and cold—have always been conjoined together; if flame or snow be presented anew to the senses, the mind is carried by custom to expect heat or cold, and to believe that such a quality does exist, and will discover itself upon a nearer approach. This belief is the necessary result of placing the mind in such circumstances. It is an operation of the soul, when we are so situated, as unavoidable as to feel the passion of love, when we receive benefits; or hatred, when we meet with injuries. All these operations are a species of natural instincts, which no reasoning or process of the thought and understanding is able either to produce or to prevent. (*Enquiry*, Section 5, Part 1)

Does not this last sentence express a view of the place of primitive unreflective response in our beliefs which is very similar to the one that we have seen Wittgenstein wishing to emphasize? Beliefs as to the effects of fire, or as to the nourishing properties of a substance, are founded on facts of human response and behaviour. There is no question of being able to give a justification for human beliefs or actions, in the sense of being able to give reasons for saying that people are *right* in believing what they believe, by appeal to arguments showing that such and such an effect *must* follow from such and such a cause. We have to rest on the fact that people do so act and believe. (See particularly *OC* 284.)

Wittgenstein seems to agree with Hume that actions or beliefs based merely on past experience cannot be justified by reference to some law of induction or of the uniformity of nature. See especially *OC* 287:

> The squirrel does not infer by induction that it is going to need stores next winter as well. And no more do we need a law of induction to justify our actions or predictions.

Hume was also at pains to point out that there could be no *a priori* basis for science. Thus, in so far as this position involves a rejection of the idea that facts about the world can be deduced from any metaphysical account of the relation of thought to reality (as Descartes held), Wittgenstein and Hume may be seen to be in agreement. But there are many points of difference.

A general difference is the difference in Hume's overall framework. Hume explicitly places the notion of a causal connection in the context of his epistemology: causality is ultimately accounted for in terms of qualities of, or relations between, ideas in the mind. But there is also a particular difference, one which has a direct bearing on certain sections in *On Certainty*.

In Section 4, Part 2 of the *Enquiry* Hume asks:

> Is there any more intelligible proposition than to affirm, that all the trees will flourish in December and January, and decay in May and June? Now whatever is intelligible and can be distinctly conceived, implies no contradiction, and can never be proved false by any demonstrative argument or abstract reasoning *a priori*.

Hume, of course, is suggesting something much more radical than that we just change the names of the months around: he is suggesting that we imagine the trees beginning a new growth-cycle at the time of year when the climatic conditions are most against it. But to take such a supposition seriously would mean supposing many other things to be different also, for the fact that the trees come into bud in March and April in the Northern Hemisphere is connected with many other climatic and natural phenomena. Any description of an object or event already includes the idea of connections between it and other objects or events. I am thinking in this connection of those sections of *On Certainty*, particularly *OC* 274, in which Wittgenstein says that a proposition which expresses a belief or describes an experience is not held or stated in isolation (cf. *OC* 141) but is 'surrounded by others which combine with it to form a system' (*OC* 603). An experience of something that has happened in the past does not, of itself, give a ground for thinking that this event will always happen in similar circumstances— that it happens according to a law of nature. Its place in a *system* of understanding or belief is also relevant. Compare the example of *OC* 240: the belief that all human beings have parents is based not only on the experience of knowing the parents of certain people, but on a whole network of other facts which have been discovered and learnt about the anatomy, physiology and sexual life of animals. But notice here that Wittgenstein, in questioning whether or not the citing of such facts constitutes a proof, speaks, like Hume, of deriving this knowledge from *one man's* experience. The branch of science dealing with human biology, like any other branch of science, forms a system of interrelated facts. But this system is not constructed on the basis of one man's experience, nor could anyone not particularly learned in human biology recount the facts in sufficient detail. In contrast with Hume's isolated man, however, who is conceived as 'coming of a sudden into this world', the individual in Wittgenstein's case is someone who belongs 'to a community which is bound together by science and education' (*OC* 298), and it is this link which dictates how he understands his experience. (I have taken this last point from *OC* 145. However, I have used the expression 'how he understands his experience' in preference to Wittgenstein's wording at *OC* 145, for the idea that one's experiences are *interpreted* suggests that there are data of experience in a general sense which are neutral as between, while common to, different interpretations. To talk in any general way about the data of experience in this sense would in fact be antipathetic to Wittgenstein's account.)

Hume claims that the fact that the same thing has happened again is not a proof that in similar circumstances it always will. And at *OC* 295 Wittgenstein agrees. But this is no reason for arguing that we have therefore no right to assume that it will. Hume's account of the way we acquire knowledge on the basis of experience of what has happened in the past is *not* in intent a sceptical one. There may be many difficulties with the way he substantiates his claim that all knowledge of fact or existence is based on a 'habit of the mind', but his insistence that a method of inductive reasoning can have no *a priori* foundation need not lead to scepticism about any of our beliefs arrived at by this method. It is Russell, in fact, who presses the sceptical point. In his chapter on induction in *The Problems of Philosophy* he writes:

> The mere fact that something has happened a certain number of times causes animals and men to expect that it will happen again. Thus our instincts certainly cause us to believe that the sun will rise to-morrow, but we may be in no better a position than the chicken which unexpectedly has its neck wrung. We have therefore to distinguish the fact that past uniformities cause expectations as to the future, from the question whether there is any reasonable ground for giving weight to such expectations after the question of their validity has been raised. (page 35)

Here Russell makes the distinction which I have said is central in philosophically sceptical arguments. He distinguishes between questioning the validity of a judgement by appeal to the grounds or criteria used to arrive at it (in this case, inductive evidence), and questioning the validity of those criteria themselves. So he sees the problem in this way:

> The problem we have to discuss is whether there is any reason for believing in what is called 'the uniformity of nature'. The belief in the uniformity of nature is the belief that everything that has happened or will happen is an instance of some general law to which there are no exceptions. (page 35)

On the answer to the question whether or not we can validate all our expectations as to the future must depend, he says, 'all the beliefs upon which our daily life is based'.

At *OC* 429 Wittgenstein asks the same question. Previous experience, he says, may very well be the *cause* of my present certitude, but is it its ground? And at *OC* 130–31 he agrees that although experience *can* be the ground for some judgements, the judgement that experience is a valid ground for judgement cannot itself be grounded in experience. This latter point Russell would agree with: it is part of his own point. We cannot appeal to experience here, on pain of defending ourselves with what we are trying to defend. At *OC* 130 Wittgenstein also says that we do not *have* a ground for regarding experience as a valid ground of judgement. However, in contrast with Russell, he does not think that this fact raises any worry as to the validity of the beliefs upon which our daily life is based: there is no question of its invalidating his belief about his toes, for instance (*OC* 429). Wittgenstein's discussion of Russell's problem is centred on *OC* 130–135 and 615–619. At *OC* 617 he asks, 'Doesn't it seem obvious that the possibility of a language-game is conditioned by certain facts?'; and I think we may take as an example the language-game envisaged in connection with *OC* 134, of asking where such and such a book is. It might seem obvious that the possibility of entering into conversation with someone about where you might find your book depends on the fact that books do not just vanish without good reason from where people put them. But if we do put the matter in this way, it looks as though that fact (that books don't just vanish, etc.) can be established, and questioned, independently of the role it plays in such a language-game. So, to use this example to fill out the argument of *OC* 168, if we say that the possibility of asking about the whereabouts of a book is conditioned by certain facts, then it would seem that the language-game must '*show*' the facts that make it possible. It would seem to have to show, for example, that the stability of books is subject to certain facts about the combustibility of paper. But this overlooks the point that what the facts actually are is *stated* in terms of concepts used according to certain rules of sense and nonsense. We establish what the facts are by a process of investigation, so we cannot appeal to these facts to validate the process. This is not to deny that we can discover facts which show that some aspect or particular method of investigation was inaccurate or misleading, but it is to deny that we can appeal to them to validate all methods or to validate the foundations of any method. Similarly, if we say that induction is possible and yields true conclusions only because there are events which occur with law-like regularity, then that there are these regular occurrences must be capable of being established independently of our use of the methods of inference.

It does happen that objects such as books disappear. But we don't say that they have just vanished away: rather, that we can't think what *must have* happened to them. In other words, there must be some explanation, only we don't know it. But in being so sure, are we making a metaphysical claim about the nature of the world, namely that it is subject to a law of the uniformity of nature? For what, substantially, would we be claiming if not something descriptive of the way we think and reason about things? Compare *OC* 135 and Wittgenstein's comparison with the squirrel at *OC* 287. A general law to the effect that nature behaves in a uniform fashion would not validate the particular laws which we have discovered, for it's only in terms of such laws that any statement about the uniform behaviour of nature has sense. Nor would an unforeseen and amazing irregularity in such laws give us reason to suppose that nature was not uniform in pattern after all. For even if it led to an enormous revision in the explanatory system (and the situations in which this does happen are far from easily specified), this would not constitute a revision of the view that nature behaves uniformly. The belief that things just don't behave in a totally erratic and unlaw-like manner, which Russell requires us to find reasons for believing, is easy to understand if it is substantiated in terms of beliefs about particular laws of behaviour of bodies. But Russell requires it to be more than this, and, in so doing, requires that we understand what it would be for something to behave in an unlaw-like manner, by which is not just meant that some irregularity or change, as yet unexplained, has occurred. The fact, however, that nothing would count as an instance of such an irregularity, and that we should even be willing radically to revise our theories according to which things do happen, makes it apparent that the question which Russell wants answered is not: how do we know that nature really is uniform? but: how do we know that our thoughts and methods of inferring the truth about things really do accord with how things are?

So far in these units, I have been trying to bring out some of the issues involved in Wittgenstein's criticism of this question—the criticism, in his terms, of the view that a language-game can, or need, have any justification. In his view, to ask that our methods of inference and grounds for judgement be justified undermines the rules and framework in terms of which *any* question of validation has sense. I have also tried to show how this view is an essential part of Wittgenstein's overall view of meaning, so that criticism of the position he takes against the sceptic will involve criticism of his view of meaning as developed in his later works. But there is a different way of approaching Wittgenstein's position: namely, to see how it arises from a certain view of *truth*. Meaning and truth are, of course, essentially connected, and so this approach involves reviewing different aspects of the same arguments, not assessing different arguments. As will be obvious from my rephrasing above, Russell's question also involves a certain view about truth: a proposition is true if it agrees with reality, or with how things are, and the methods we use to arrive at some proposition are valid in so far as they arrive at a proposition which can be seen to be true. The first part of this view is, taken simply, uncontentious; it is the second part against which many of Wittgenstein's remarks in *On Certainty* are directed. This question I will take up in section 5.

4.5 SYSTEM AND SCIENCE

I have indicated at various points that Wittgenstein places great emphasis on the fact that a person's beliefs, doubts and judgements form a *system*, a system which he shares with others. If I doubt (e.g. *OC* 126), or believe (e.g. *OC* 141), some proposition, then the fact that I do so brings into question, or commits me to affirm, many others. (Cf. *OC* 255.) Similarly, a judgement does not stand or fall in isolation from all others. There are some beliefs which I shall not give up, despite all evidence to the contrary at some particular instant, for to do so would involve giving up an entire system of beliefs: rather, I shall judge that I was hallucinating, or that the evidence was in some way unknown to me or misleading (*OC* 636). For example, even though I might find a liquid which seemed to have all the properties of water, except that it did not boil at 100°C, this would not disprove any law of physics, even if I repeated the finding several times as 'an experiment' (see *OC* 603–04).

In *On Certainty*, Wittgenstein leaves the notion of a system very vague. And it is partly this vagueness, as we shall see in section 5, that has provoked much criticism. Crucial questions arise about the connection or lack of connection between different systems, which cannot adequately be dealt with unless one has a clearer idea of Wittgenstein's use of the notion. These questions also arise in connection with related notions, such as 'language game', 'practice', a 'world-view' and a 'framework of belief', all of which occur in *On Certainty*. One thing which is particularly open to dispute is the way in which these different notions are interrelated. It must be the case, I think, that a system is wider in scope than a language-game, since a system of belief and enquiry, such as the system of scientific belief, involves many different language-games. Further, a language-game is to be distinguished from a practice, in that one and the same language-game, say that of asking for a certain physical object, can run through many different practices, e.g. building or surgery. Different language-games and different practices, then, cannot be discontinuous or unconnected.

There are two ways, however, in which Wittgenstein is *not* using the notion of a system: firstly, in the sense in which the whole of *language* is to be understood primarily as a truth-functionally connected system of propositions (as in the *Tractatus*, for example); secondly, in the sense in which *knowledge* is a system of truths, all derived in the same manner from some basic set of propositions (in the classical Cartesian or empiricist sense).

Descartes' picture of the house of knowledge involved, as we have seen, a structure in which the different areas of knowledge were ordered hierarchically, proceeding from truths which could be specified and established as true independently of their relation to any other truths of the structure. At *OC* 102 Wittgenstein also speaks of a person's convictions as fitting together into a structure, and at *OC* 410 he says that our knowledge—as a whole—forms *an* enormous system. In his speaking of *one man's* convictions and of *our* system of knowledge there seems to be room for comparing one man's system with another's and our system of knowledge with that of some other group. At *OC* 410, however, following his remark that knowledge forms a system, he speaks about the entire *system of language-games*. It is clear from this, and from the central role played by the notion of a language-game in his remarks on knowledge and certainty, that he does not see knowledge as forming a system in the sense that its different areas or subjects are ordered hierarchically or in any other way, and that he does not think that one man can build a system of knowledge in isolation from others: even though two men may know different sets of facts, they share a common method of establishing the facts. And at *OC* 141, after speaking of 'a whole system of propositions', he goes on to deny that in the system it is single axioms that strike one as obvious, as was the case in Descartes' account; in contrast, consequences and premises give one another *mutual* support. This point of contrast is repeated at *OC* 152. The propositions which stand fast in the system of knowledge are not fixed in the sense that anything holds them fast—that is, they are not, in Descartes' sense, logically indubitable or logically guaranteed—but the other things we can do and say determine that they stand fast. For Wittgenstein, then, the relationship of the foundations to the other parts of the system is different; the 'empirical propositions' do not form a homogeneous mass (*OC* 213), in the sense not only that they are not all susceptible of being tested by the same method, but that they are not *all* equally subject to testing (*OC* 162).

As we saw in section 4, some empirical propositions, such as those enumerated by Moore, play a logical role in any method of testing, and so are themselves not subject to testing. At *OC* 167 Wittgenstein puts this by saying that an empirical proposition can be turned into a norm of description. His example is from science. In the context of a scientific investigation there are strict rules as to what is going to count as an example of a substance, so that substances can be quite strictly defined as being subject to certain laws. Such laws, and propositions stating what are the discoverable facts about substances, can be turned into norms of description. As such, they will play a constitutive role in the *method* of our investigation. However, there is no strict boundary between the laws which play such a role and the laws or facts we discover through using them. Furthermore, what constitutes a rule of investigation or norm of testing in one enquiry may become the subject of investigation in another. This is again relevant to Wittgenstein's image of the river and the river-bed at *OC* 96–97. (You may have recognized that the issues here are the same as those raised by Locke when he distinguishes between the real and nominal essence of a substance.)

As far as the context of science is concerned, it may be said that any proposition or empirical description can be transformed into a postulate—so that it then becomes a norm of description. What is relevant is the role the proposition plays in the theory. But when Wittgenstein does actually say this, at *OC* 321, he goes on to say that he has reservations about this way of putting it. He had preceded this remark by reminding the reader that the concept 'proposition' itself is not a sharp one. Again, this way of putting the matter is misleading; it is too reminiscent of the *Tractatus* programme of providing a general account of the proposition as part of an overall theory of language. On the later account, you cannot give any general characterization, even a formal one, of the propositions which are norms of description or method. As I mentioned in section 1, the fact that science deals with what can be quantified and measured has a lot to do with the fact that it is often put forward as a paradigm of an *objective* study: the results arrived at in any investigation can be tested and confirmed by anyone trained in the methods. And as I mentioned above, there are strict rules and procedures for isolating the substances or relations investigated. It is these features of scientific method which underlie the idea that science gives us a more exact or accurate picture of the world.

In Units 3–4, Susan Khin Zaw presented Locke's philosophy, which with Descartes' laid the foundations for modern Western philosophy, as a way of dealing with the new methods and findings of the new science. In her section 1.4 she says that the Galilean system represented nothing less than the beginning of a new conception of reality in which, through the use, for example, of such concepts as *temperature*, as distinct from *heat* and *cold* (which are derived from *the way things feel to me*), we can invoke the *objective truth* about substances. So, in our commerce with the world, the development of the new methods of science leads to the idea that 'objective truth begins to have the edge over subjective judgement', as Susan Khin Zaw puts it (Units 3–4, page 17). This idea she describes as 'the metaphysical bias of our time'. In so far as it is meaningful to talk of accuracy in connection with such a generalization, I think that this is an accurate description of the impulse and development of Western thought.

As you saw in Units 11–13, positivism, which has had a wide influence in contemporary philosophy, saw philosophy as consisting primarily of the philosophy of science: the propositions of science were presented as paradigms of significant discourse. There are many philosophers still working in the tradition of positivism who largely equate philosophy with the philosophy of science. In 1960, for instance, the American philosopher W. V. O. Quine published a very influential book, *Word and Object*, in which he said:

> What reality is like is the business of scientists, in the broadest sense, painstakingly to surmise; and what there is, what is real, is part of that question. The question how we know what there is is simply part of the question...of the evidence for truth about the world. The last arbiter is so-called scientific method, however amorphous.[1]

And in the 1970s there has been a great deal of argument in support of materialism, the view held, for instance, by J. J. C. Smart (one of the leading exponents of this position) that 'there is nothing in the universe over and above the entities postulated by physics. To explain the facts about the universe, including living creatures both human and non-human, there is no obstacle (other than the finiteness of our minds, and our inevitable ignorance) to the programme of using a mixture of natural history on the one hand, and physics and chemistry on the other.'

Thus there is much support in contemporary philosophy, in varying degrees of sophistication, for the view that science, or the sciences, provide us with a comprehensive system of knowledge. On this view, any claim or belief which is incompatible with the truths of science is false, and, on some

---

[1] MIT Press, page 22.

interpretations, any statement of belief which is not susceptible of enquiry by the methods of science is meaningless. (You studied the roots of such a view in Units 11–13.)

At *OC* 298 Wittgenstein acknowledges and accepts the pervasive influence of science in our dealings with the world, and at *OC* 324 he equates what is *reasonable* with what is compatible with scientific evidence. However, when he speaks of our beliefs, doubts and judgements forming a system, he cannot be identifying this system with the system of science, for the idea that there is a unitary way of understanding the world and our interactions with it and with each other is in direct opposition to his view that modes of understanding, and the varieties of sorts of things which can be understood, are as various as the language-games in which we can speak of knowledge, understanding and explanation. *Explaining* something in terms of theories and laws established by scientific method is but one way in which a person can relate to the world. It is a significant implication, for instance, of Wittgenstein's emphasis on the *rule-governed* aspect of human behaviour in his later works that an explanation of human activity cannot be given by reference to a set of causal laws which takes no account of the concepts used by people engaged in the activity to describe their motivations, reasons and intentions. (For an expansion of this point, see the book by P. Winch listed in the bibliography, and for a criticism of this view, Gellner's article 'The New Idealism'.)

Wittgenstein's conception of knowledge, then, can be seen to be fighting against the 'metaphysical bias of our time' inasmuch as Wittgenstein repeatedly emphasizes the diversity of human practices and areas of discourse. So although, as we have seen, he does speak at *OC* 141 of 'the whole system of propositions', this must be put against his insistence that there is no unitary concept of a proposition and that the sorts of things we can assert and the grounds on which we can do so are extremely diverse. Indeed, at several places he gives examples of *different* systems. He speaks, for instance, of a colour system and a number system; at *OC* 108 he speaks of our system of physics and it is possible, from his remark at *OC* 107, that he also sees religious belief as forming a system.

I think it is obvious from several of the remarks of *On Certainty* that what Wittgenstein has in mind, when using the term 'system' in these contexts, is a system of evidence and verification; the methods of confirmation and enquiry that are applicable in one area are not applicable in another. (See, for instance, *OC* 105.) Thus, when at *OC* 102 Wittgenstein speaks of something's not 'fitting into' our system of convictions, we might cite the example of someone like Yuri Geller, who claims to be able to manipulate metals in ways which do not fit, or accord with, the laws of science. We do not know where to 'put' the event he is apparently bringing about; we do not know what to connect it up with. There are two alternatives: either we can dismiss his activities (and possibly question his integrity) by saying that we don't know how he does it but that it must be by some means compatible with the laws of science, or we can be agnostic until such time as the system of connections has shifted in terms of which we attempt to understand what he is doing. Some people, by invoking the concepts involved in the area of ESP, would claim that we already have a system in which a description of such happenings has a place.

If we are to accept this picture of knowledge as consisting of different systems of belief, in the sense that geography, history, medicine and religion, for example, form different systems of evidence and verification whose rules depend upon the sort of thing investigated in each case, then these systems cannot be thought of as discrete and discontinuous: facts established in, say, history or biology can influence what is believed in medicine or religion. (For instance, Darwinian thought had a great impact on religious belief.) But emphasizing the fact that there are different systems brings into prominence the fact that there is no one way in which the facts in the different areas *must* be seen to be related. A religious believer need not give up his beliefs in the face of Darwin's discoveries on grounds of inconsistency, though he may be required to modify them. One of the main points, then, about Wittgenstein's use of the notion of a system is, as I see it, that propositions are not believed in isolation from one another, but that the ways in which we see the connections between them cannot be stated in any formula which prescribes that they *must* be seen in one way rather than in another. A radical change in any system of belief, then, either in a personal sense or in the sense in which Newton's or Freud's ideas brought about such a change, involves the possibility of seeing the facts as connected in a different way, which, in turn, introduces the possibility of discovering different facts.

At *OC* 144, Wittgenstein mentions the fact that the beliefs of a system can change and shift. His own case of believing that it is impossible for anyone to go to the moon serves as an example. At *OC* 108, he says that our whole system of physics forbids us to believe this. Here is one case, at least, in which Wittgenstein was obviously too conservative in his beliefs about what is possible. But this conservatism is not entailed by his epistemology, for he goes on to show that it is precisely in terms of the 'system of physics' that we could come to understand just how it *would be* possible. A physicist *would* be able to answer the questions following his remark at *OC* 108. The beliefs of one person's system, then, can change, and the relative emphasis of each of his beliefs can shift, when he learns more or sees connections between different areas of his experience which he had previously not seen.

Wittgenstein does not take on in any direct way these questions of the interrelationships of systems of belief. However, there are several remarks in *On Certainty* criticizing someone who, unlike Wittgenstein, sees the system of science as a *comprehensive* system and so has to face no such questions. Such a person would claim to have a method for testing the validity or intelligibility of any claim in any area. That is, he could say that a belief either 'tallies with the facts or it doesn't' *and* that we have in science a method for establishing just what the facts are, a method which distinguishes myths and superstitions from genuine beliefs. He could say to Wittgenstein, as is said at *OC* 595, that the beliefs of someone who engaged in a practice such as tribal witchcraft, for example, may connect together into a system and yet that 'none of these beliefs correspond with reality'.

It is these issues which I shall deal with in section 5.

4.6   A NOTE ON WITTGENSTEIN AND QUINE

In Units 11–13 (pp. 64–65), a comparison is made between certain of the things Wittgenstein says about a body of knowledge, and what is said by W. V. O. Quine. I have already mentioned the fact that Quine's view of the unitary structure of knowledge and his equation of philosophy with the philosophy of science place him in opposition to Wittgenstein, but Quine's comparison (taken from Neurath) of the body of knowledge to a ship at sea which has to be repaired whilst afloat has many features in common with ideas put forward in *On Certainty*. Quine, like Wittgenstein, opposes the traditional empiricist programme of attempting to display the foundations upon which all knowledge must ultimately rest: the programme of construction from, or reduction to, epistemological foundations cannot be carried through. He also thinks it is 'folly to seek a boundary between synthetic statements, which hold contingently on experience, and analytic statements which hold come what may',[1] a position which has similarities to Wittgenstein's view at *OC* 318. Again, Quine says that the truth of any statement cannot be considered in isolation from others: 'Re-evaluation of some statements entails re-evaluation of others, because of their logical interconnections—the logical laws being in turn simply certain further statements of the system.' He maintains that no statement is immune from revision. And, like Wittgenstein at *OC* 92, he cites simplicity as a criterion for the correctness of a view. All these points, then, have parallels in the picture presented by Wittgenstein.

Yet Wittgenstein's reluctance (*OC* 321) to say that 'any empirical proposition can, theoretically be transformed...', marks a serious difference. He asks what 'theoretically' can mean here. Well, one thing it can mean is the sort of view which Quine held in 'Two Dogmas of Empiricism'. Quine there said that physical objects are *posited* to expedite our dealings with sense experience. The question whether there are such things as physical objects is on a par with questions of natural science. They are the *posits of a theory*. So *theoretically*, any statement can be held true come what may, if we make drastic enough adjustments in the system. Wittgenstein's second remark at *OC* 410 sounds as though it has affinities with this part of Quine's picture: as though it is up to us to choose, in accordance with the principles of simplicity and expedience, what status we give to some particular proposition. Yet for Wittgenstein to say this would go against his explicit rejection of the idea that statements about physical objects are in any sense *posits* or hypotheses put forward in order to explain or in any sense 'deal with' sense experience. Furthermore, although there may be no empirical propositions about which we are infallible and which are immune from revision in any context. Wittgenstein makes much of the fact that there are constraints on what we can believe or consider, namely the constraints on what we find it possible to *do*.

[1] The references to Quine are to his article 'Two Dogmas of Empiricism', in *From A Logical Point of View*, Harper Torchbooks, 1963, pp. 42 ff; part of this article is reprinted in Units 11–13, pp. 64–65.

5.1 TRUTH AND AGREEMENT WITH REALITY

In these units I have presented the sceptic as one who calls in question the propriety of saying the kinds of things we do about material objects, about another person's feelings, or about events which happened in the past or will happen in the future. In particular, he questions the validity of any judgement we can make about such matters and so undermines our confidence that there is any genuine distinction between truth and falsity here at all. I have also said that calling judgements into question in this way leads to the demand for some *justification* for speaking as we do about such matters, and leads to a demand for justification of the methods of evidence we use to determine the truth or falsity of any such judgement. I presented the attempt to meet this demand as the attempt to give a guarantee that there are such things as material objects, or whatever, for us to speak about, by showing how judgements about them are logically related to other, more fundamental or basic judgements, which are infallible.

I have also attempted in these units to bring out some of the questions involved in Wittgenstein's refusal to meet the demand for such a justification. His refusal to do so is, in fact, continuous with his position in the *Tractatus*: according to the *Tractatus* (e.g. *T*4.1272) there can be no meaningful question raised as to whether or not the 'objects' which correlate with the names of a proposition exist. This position has a formal similarity to the view in *On Certainty* that questions or assertions about the existence of material objects as such cannot be raised or confirmed. A word naming an object cannot be *justified* by our pointing to what it names. But the views of meaning and truth involved in the two works are very different.

In the later work, the signs of a proposition, or the signs used in fact-stating discourse, derive meaning, not by correlation with objects, but by being used according to a method. In the *Tractatus* the truth of an empirical proposition lies in its correspondence with reality. Now this view does capture something essential to any account of truth, namely that it is the facts which constrain any judgement about what is true. But any general elucidation of the view that truth consists of a relation between language and reality is complicated by the fact that any description of reality, or the facts, is given *in language*. I said towards the end of section 4 that Russell's question whether our ways of speaking and methods of judging really do accord with how things are, presumes a certain view of truth: namely, that a proposition is true if it agrees will reality, *and* that we can give a general specification of the constituents of reality. If one's emphasis is epistemological and empiricist, as is the case with Russell, these constituents will be the ultimately simple elements given in perception. If one's emphasis is more logical, or ontological, as is the case with some of Plato's dialogues or Wittgenstein's *Tractatus*, they will be certain objects characterized as unchanging or eternal. In either case, such things are supposed to provide an anchoring-point both for the meaning and for the truth of what we say, outside language. *Wittgenstein, in his later writings, rejects this picture of language as anchored or justified in either of these metaphysical senses.* I say 'metaphysical', in order to contrast what he rejects with what he obviously accepts: namely, that what justifies my saying that the sun has come out is the fact that it has. The fact that the sun has come out is not an event in language. But the statement of this fact, of course, is.

Wittgenstein does not deny that a proposition is true if it agrees with, or corresponds to, a fact, if this just means that, *for example*, 'the sun is shining' is true if the sun is in fact shining. But he denies that this account could be an adequate basis for a *theory of truth*, for he denies that any *general* account can be given of the relation between a proposition and a fact. The remarks in *On Certainty* that relate directly to this occur between *OC* 191 and *OC* 204.

At *OC* 191 he raises the question, 'Does some proposition which we unquestioningly acknowledge as true actually agree with reality?' and says that with this question 'you are already going round in a circle'. At *OC* 203 he raises the same question and concludes that the agreement consists in the fact that the proposition is true if the evidence supports it. If we put these two remarks together, we can see that the question is circular because we are at one and the same time asking whether a proposition (which has been arrived at on the basis of some method of enquiry and system of evidence) agrees with the facts, and saying that what the facts *are* are the facts as they have been established in terms of some method of enquiry and system of evidence. To invoke 'reality' as a test of the correctness of the method of evidence *is* to bring in those facts established within the method. So, on Wittgenstein's view, what makes a judgement true is the fact *as it is established by the evidence*, not something further like 'agreement with reality'.

At the end of *OC* 203 Wittgenstein refers in parenthesis to the *Tractatus*. In the *Tractatus* he speaks of a proposition's being true or false in virtue of its being a picture of reality, and he says that the picture or proposition is laid against reality *like a measure* (*T* 2.1512). How do you think this image, that establishing the truth of a proposition is like laying a measure against an object, contrasts with the closing remarks of *OC* 203 and *OC* 200?

In the *Tractatus* it was thought that, given *the* correct analysis of a proposition, there was no problem about what the agreement of a proposition with reality would be. The agreement or disagreement of a proposition's sense with a fact constituted its truth or falsity. A proposition is true if, when it is compared with reality, the elements of the proposition are related to one another in the same way as the objects of a fact are related. And since the proposition has a sense, there must be some unchanging constituents of reality with which the names constituting the proposition can be correlated. To test whether a proposition agrees with reality one 'lays it against it like a measure' and sees whether the elements of the proposition—by analogy with the 'graduating lines' or units of measurement of the measuring instrument—correlate with the objects in reality (*T* 2.1512–2.16).

This image is helpful, however, only in so far as we accept the theory that there *are* constituents of the proposition, and constituents of reality, that can be marked off, on a one-to-one basis, in this way. But speaking in this general way of the constituents of a proposition and the constituents of reality bypasses completely any reference to *how* the proposition-reality comparison is made and gives the impression that ascertaining the truth of a proposition always consists in the same simple operation. On the *Tractatus* account, a proposition is in agreement with reality if the proposition and the fact have the same structural arrangement. But what counts as the same structure? We might possibly say of an object one metre long that the metre ruler and the object 'share the same length', but whether or not a ruler is the same length as an object depends on there being a *method* of comparing lengths. The simile that a proposition is like a measure that can be applied to reality seems unproblematic, because we all know what to do when asked to measure an object with a ruler, but it is unhelpful if, on the analogy with truth, the question is a request for some account of measuring.

At the end of *OC* 203 Wittgenstein says that a proposition is true if it is supported by whatever sort of evidence (evidence in the 'language-game') is appropriate to deciding for or against it. But what count as the appropriate evidence and as the correct methods used to establish it—that is, what the grounds are for deciding for or against a proposition—differ from case to case (*OC* 200). By contrast with the picture presented in the *Tractatus*, Wittgenstein's later account stresses that establishing the truth of a proposition is the result of a process or method, and that there are many different methods. If we reapply the measuring image to this later view, we must say that determining the length of an object with a measuring instrument involves mastering the technique of application of the instrument, since determining whether a proposition is true or not involves establishing and assessing the evidence. The simple operation of 'looking and seeing' requires that you know what you are looking for, and is often merely the final stage of a long *process* of arranging and uncovering what there is to be seen. Think, for example, of the techniques which have to be mastered before the truth of a diagnosis of a person's state of health—physical or mental—can be established.

In terms of the analogy with measuring, it's what you *do* with the ruler that determines whether you get this result or that, and—to invoke again a central concept in Wittgenstein's account of meaning and truth—whether you get the *correct* result depends on there being *agreement in the methods of measuring*. (I emphasize once more that this does not mean that we simply come to some agreement about the methods we use, in the way that we have agreed, for example, to adopt the convention of using the metric system; rather, if there is to *be* any method or technique, then there must be agreement in its application.) There is a passage in the *Philosophical Investigations* which briefly discusses the notion of establishing the length of an object and which can be read on the analogy of establishing the truth of a proposition:

> One judges the length of a rod and can look for and find some method of judging it more exactly or more reliably. So—you say—*what* is judged here is independent of the method of judging it. What length *is* cannot be defined by the method of determining length.—To think like this is to make a mistake. What mistake? To say 'The height of Mont Blanc depends on how one climbs it' would be queer. And one wants to compare 'ever more accurate measurement of length' with the nearer and nearer approach to an object. But in certain cases it is, and in certain cases it is *not*, clear what 'approaching nearer to the length of an object' means. What 'determining the length' means is not learned by learning what *length* and *determining* are; the meaning of the word 'length' is learnt by learning, among other things, what it is to determine length. (*PI* II, xi, page 225).

The question whether or not the methods we use to determine the truth of a proposition do really arrive at the truth, so that what is determined really does 'agree with reality', is parallel to the question, 'Are our ways of measuring the *correct* ones?' The question suggests that there is a notion of the correct results, or the facts, existing independently of any method used to arrive at them. There are various ways of measuring the area of a field, for instance: using sophisticated land-surveying equipment, striding it out, measuring it in terms of the time it takes a man to plough it. Which is the correct method? It is tempting to say that the first method will provide the correct results because it is a 'more accurate measurement of area': as though the precision of the instruments used gets 'nearer to' the 'actual size' of the field. And for *certain purposes*, this technique is more accurate. But the other methods are not *wrong*, nor are the results arrived at by using them, if they are applied with care and deliberation only *approximate*. The correct results are those arrived at by the proper application of a particular method, and the notion of precision is the notion of what counts as precise application in each case. Similarly, the truth about a man's behaviour is not more accurately ascertained, is not characterized in closer accordance with 'the facts' or 'reality', by a method which investigates his neural and physiological processes than it is by a method which enquires into his motives and beliefs. Two different sorts of things are being found out about his behaviour in the two cases.

5.2 VERIFICATIONISM AND IDEALISM

The remarks of the previous sub-section may sound to you somewhat reminiscent of the verificationist thesis that the meaning or sense of a proposition is given in terms of its method, or techniques, or verification: that the meaning of the proposition 'This object is such and such a length', for example, is given in terms of the methods used to measure the object.[1] And on page 225 of the *Investigations* Wittgenstein does say that the meaning of the word 'length' is learnt by learning, among other things, what it is to determine length. In that paragraph of the *Investigations* he may seem to be defending the verificationist thesis, in so far as he is opposing a 'realist' view that what is judged (here, 'length'), exists independently of the method of judging it. Wittgenstein says that this is a mistaken view. He is not, however, saying it is mistaken on the grounds that one ought to say, for example, 'The height of Mt. Blanc depends on how one climbs it'. Those who advocate some version of a strong verificationist thesis are, I think, committed to saying something as odd as this, because such a thesis construes the meaning of a proposition *exclusively* in terms, not simply of methods of determining its truth, but of some particular method. Wittgenstein is in agreement with the verificationist thesis, however, only in so far as it denies that the notion of 'length' has any sense independently of techniques of measuring things and that the notions of 'the truth', or 'the facts', have a sense that is altogether independent of the means of establishing them. This does not commit him to the view that how long something is depends on how one measures it, or that what is true (what the facts are) depends on how one establishes it. Rather, the methods determine the *sense of the concepts* used to state the length or describe the facts.

But the fundamental difference between Wittgenstein's position and that of verificationism is the fact that the verificationist thesis is a thesis about meaning which puts central emphasis on the notion of a proposition and the correlative notion of truth. Some commentators and critics of Wittgenstein's later views have said that he gives an account of truth in terms, not of *truth-conditions*, but of *assertion-conditions*. In the *Tractatus*, sentences expressing a proposition have meaning in virtue of their truth-conditions—i.e., the conditions in virtue of which the proposition is true or false. A verificationist

---

[1] One article which argues that Wittgenstein is committed to some version of verificationism—in the form of operationalism and logical behaviourism—is to be found in the set book *Wittgenstein* edited by Pitcher: 'Operationalism and Ordinary Language, A Critique of Wittgenstein' by C. S. Chihara and J. A. Fodor.

thesis, on the other hand, replaces truth-conditions here with assertion-conditions—i.e. the conditions which determine whether or not it is appropriate to assert a given sentence. These issues and their relation to Wittgenstein,—in particular to his use of the notion of a *criterion*, which to some has looked very like some philosophers' use of the notion of assertion-conditions[1]—are the main topics of the final unit of the course. I think it is sufficient to note here that the terminology of truth-conditions and assertion-conditions actually belongs to a view of meaning which is to be distinguished from Wittgenstein's, namely one which sees *truth* as the fundamental concept in any account of meaning. Wittgenstein does not replace truth-conditions with assertion-conditions, for his view is that the notion of meaning is not to be elucidated in terms of a general theory of truth at all. Nor does he *replace* the concept of truth with the concept of *use*; his emphasis on the use to which any utterance is put in any discourse or activity does not enable any systematic account of the meaning of any utterance to be given. Finally, it is misleading to assimilate his use of the notion of 'criterion' to that of 'assertion-conditions', since this obscures the fact that 'inner processes' (such as pains, sensations and feelings) are not *identical* with their 'outer criteria' (viz., the behaviour someone manifests). How someone behaves is a criterion for the use of a concept such as 'pain' in any claim about what he is feeling, but there is a grammatical difference between the way in which we speak of someone's behaviour and the way in which we speak of his pain; that is, we can say certain things about the one which it does not make sense to say about the other. So, similarly, there is a difference between what we can say about a fact and about its method of verification.

As I mentioned on page 17, the verificationist position is an anti-realist account of meaning. One reason why Wittgenstein's account has been misleadingly assimilated to that of the verificationists is that a passage such as that on page 225 of the *Investigations* is opposed to a realist position, in so far as it is opposed to the claim that we should evaluate the ways in which we describe, classify and investigate the facts about things according to whether or not these ways correctly reflect the real nature of things. Now, although Wittgenstein's own remarks (Z 413–16) about the difference between realism and idealism being merely one of battle-cry are relevant here, to those who think that the issues are usefully thought of in terms of realism and anti-realism, Wittgenstein's position does have certain characteristics of idealism. One very interesting discussion of this question is to be found in the article by Bernard Williams, 'Wittgenstein and Idealism', in the set book *Understanding Wittgenstein*. Williams suggests that Wittgenstein's account of language

> shows us everything as it appears to our interests, our concerns, our activities, though in the only sense in which we could meaningfully say that they determined everything, that statement would be false. The fact that in this way everything can be expressed only via human interests and concerns, things which are expressions of mind, and which themselves cannot ultimately be explained in any further terms: that provides grounds, I suggest, for calling such a view a kind of *idealism*.

Another philosopher who has taken Wittgenstein to be advocating a sophisticated form of idealism is Ernest Gellner. In particular, Gellner has criticized Wittgenstein's ideas as applied to issues in the social sciences, in a paper called 'The New Idealism' (published in *Positivism and Sociology*, ed. A. Giddens, Heinemann, 1974).

[1] For example, see P. M. S. Hacker, *Insight and Illusion*, as quoted in Units 11–13, page 81.

5.3 TRUTH AND 'OUR SYSTEM'

In criticizing the limitations of the view that we can account for the truth of a proposition by saying that it agrees with the facts, Wittgenstein has emphasized that 'the facts' here are the facts as they are established in terms of some *system* of enquiry and evidence. In deciding what is true we sometimes appeal, not to the immediate facts before us, but to others that we already accept. For instance, a particular perception of an object apparently freely rising into the air does not necessarily negate a belief in the laws of gravity: we sometimes question the perception on the basis of the other things we believe—that is, we assess it in relation to a system of other beliefs.

At *OC* 105 Wittgenstein says explicitly that all testing and confirmation take place within a system. However, at *OC* 107 he says that someone who holds to the belief that there is a God can give supporting grounds for his belief, *but that so can someone who does not believe.* The suggestion is that these different beliefs have their place in different systems of training: one system in which connections[1] are made between a person's experiences which provide grounds for a belief in God, and one in which they are not. This suggestion immediately invites the question whether there are any means of *objectively* deciding for or against a judgement, in the sense of deciding between two systems. In the section following (*OC* 108, which we mentioned on page 69) Wittgenstein raises this question in terms of the question, is it true or false that someone has been on the moon? His reply, as we have seen, is that, *if we are thinking within our system,* then it is certain that no-one has been on the moon. Ignoring the fact that he was wrong, in the sense of being ignorant, about the possibility of going to the moon, his answer still leaves open the issue whether or not a particular system of belief is the correct one. The issue certainly seems to make sense, arising as it does from the remarks of *OC* 107. I think we should therefore consider the question of *OC* 108, 'Is there no objective truth?' Please stop for a while to consider your own views on the question of what you would take as *objective* standards for judgement and note down your ideas as to what makes them objective. What sorts of things could we be saying, for instance, if we called someone's opinion or claim 'merely subjective'?

One possible standard of objectivity for judgements which has been rejected throughout *On Certainty* is that a judgement is objectively certain if it concerns something about which the speaker could not be wrong, in virtue of some special feature of the proposition judged. Examples would be necessary truths, first-person reports of states of mind, and statements which are peculiarly validated in the utterance of them (such as Descartes' *cogito*). This standard of objective certainty is a philosophical one, which radically limits, and is at odds with, what we ordinarily take to be objective judgement.

There is a second way, however, in which this idea of objective truth might be understood, one which, although it is related to the first, arises from different sorts of considerations. You may have thought of the cases in which we say that someone's judgement is merely subjective, meaning that it is made only from his point of view, or based only on his personal or limited experience, or based on facts which are facts about him rather than about the subject of his judgement. For instance, someone can like a certain piece

---

[1] For the importance of the idea of 'seeing connections' in Wittgenstein's work, see the article by Stuart Brown in the appendix to these units.

of music because of the personal associations which it has for him, and judge
it to be good on that basis. Someone, on the other hand, who bases his
judgement on features of the music such as its structure, development or
instrumental colour or texture is said to be making a more objective
judgement. The distinction here could be said to be a distinction between
judgements based on *features of the judging subject* and judgements based on
features of the object. Now, I think this distinction takes us straight into
interesting territory. For the question is, can the distinction be made clearly?
That is, can any general account be given of what sorts of things fall on one
side of the distinction or the other? In the musical example I said that the
judgement of the music was *subjective* if it was based on grounds which were
facts about the person making the judgement—that is, if it was based on
facts describing his personal relationship to the music. However, it might be
said that *any* grounds for making a judgement about music, or indeed any
judgements of value, are based upon the facts of how people relate to art or
to their projects and place in the world. That is (in terms of the musical
example), *facts about the music*, such as its tonal colour, are grounds for an
evaluative judgement only in so far as it is a *fact about humans* that they
respond to a given organization of sound in certain sorts of ways. And a
question whether there can be any standards of objective judgement in areas
in which values are concerned—aesthetics, ethics or religion, for
instance—then arises, from the fact that different people, or groups of
people, respond to situations differently. Arguments for an objective standard
of what is just or beautiful can, accordingly, take the form of giving reasons
which make no reference to what anyone in particular, or even people in
general, feel or want. The sceptical position corresponding to this view,
which denies the possibility of such a standard, is often described as
subjectivist.

But the distinction between features of the judging subject and features or
qualities of the object judged is difficult to make, even in those cases where
no reference need be made to values or what anyone feels, wants or needs:
that is, in cases of simply perceiving an object. It may seem that, if an object
is described as being of a certain shape or colour or size or temperature,
then, especially if the object is natural rather than man-made, some feature
of the object in itself is being described. But, as we have seen, many
philosophers and scientists have wanted to distinguish between those features
of the object which are really qualities of the object (its primary qualities)
and those which are as they are because of the way the object affects the
perceiver (the secondary qualities). We have also seen that some philosophers
have wanted to say, even more radically, that any description of an object
depends on facts about the point of view or condition of the perceiver.

Here again, then, we have an opposition between realism and idealism. As
you saw from the early part of the course, Descartes and Locke, who upheld
the distinction between primary and secondary qualities, were both realists,
and Berkeley's criticism and rejection of the distinction is a significant part of
his arguments in favour of idealism. As I suggested in section 1, the
distinction between primary and secondary qualities is one of the sources of
the view that science gives us an objective picture of the world. And as I
added in section 4, the results obtained in science are also objective in the
sense that a properly conducted experiment eliminates, as far as possible, all
contingent variables. A question of the objectivity of experiments conducted
in the human sciences can arise because the relationship between the
experimental subject and the scientist is not always a quantifiable, or
eliminable, factor. But to the extent that science provides methods of
establishing facts about things in the world independently of man's

relationship to them, it is tempting to say that the picture of the world as given in scientific enquiry is the right one.

I think that this view is correct inasmuch as the scientific method does provide *an* objective standard and is the appropriate one to apply in many areas and situations. Science can be seen as a paradigm of objective enquiry in that, within it, rules governing what counts as *agreement in method of enquiry* are made quite explicit. The idea of an independent reality, which we can investigate and about which we can make discoveries, presupposes rules that, in principle, *anyone* can observe and methods that in principle, anyone can follow. But I think the picture of science as *the* standard for objective judgement can be misleading: firstly, if it exaggerates the extent to which the facts are established independently of man's relation to them (the focus of his attention and his use of instruments partly determine the direction and content of scientific enquiry) and, secondly, if it proposes to offer a standard of objectivity that overrules all other means of acquiring reliable and useful knowledge. (Gellner, in the article mentioned earlier, does seem to speak of science and objectivity in this way.)

At *OC* 94 Wittgenstein says that a picture of the world is neither arrived at nor held because it is established as the correct one; rather, it is inherited. To say this may seem to be bypassing the question of correctness and to be dealing instead with how the picture of the world is acquired. Yet the last part of the remark in this section—that my picture of the world is the background against which I distinguish between true and false—shows that the *question whether or not the system is correct* has no application.

In section 4 I said that Wittgenstein believed that the sorts of propositions which Moore had enumerated played a logical role in any system of judgement. When people question an entire system of belief (for instance, the system of astrology), they characteristically do so by saying that the propositions which play this logical role (for instance, the belief, in astrology, that the stars influence human affairs) are *false*. On the other hand, for those who do guide their lives in a serious and pervasive way according to the findings of astrology, that there is such an influence is not brought into question. Rather, any question of truth or falsity is raised against the background of this belief.

At *OC* 83 Wittgenstein says that the *truth* of certain empirical propositions belongs to our frame of reference. He is speaking again of the sorts of proposition which Moore enumerated, for example (*OC* 84) that the earth existed long before Moore's birth. This proposition can be contrasted with the example of *OC* 85, 'The earth has existed for such and such a length of time'. For this second proposition is only known (*if* it is known by anyone) by those who have devised methods for measuring the age of the earth, or who have been told of the results of such methods. But the sense of such techniques and activities, and *hence* (since they amount to the same thing) the sense of statements made during and arising from such techniques and activities, rest on the fact that statements such as 'The earth has existed long before my birth' are unquestionable. So when Wittgenstein says that the truth of our propositions belongs to our frame of reference, it is not the case that what we believe to be facts in geology, cosmology or history can *confirm* that the earth existed long before Moore's birth; rather, such a proposition lies at the foundation of anything we can confirm or question in the systems of scientific, historical, or other enquiries. This also supports my previous suggestion that Wittgenstein acknowledges that a system, in the narrow sense of a system of physics, or even of a system of science, is not discrete. One and the same proposition about the earth lies at the basis of many systems.

(Wittgenstein has several remarks about the relation of historical enquiry and other areas of knowledge to the existence of the earth: at *OC* 182–190, *OC* 233–238 and *OC* 310–316.)

At *OC* 253 Wittgenstein says that at the foundation of any well-founded belief (for example, a belief about a historical person such as Napoleon) lies a belief that is not founded (for example, the belief that the earth existed at the time). His remark at *OC* 83, then, goes against his remark at *OC* 205: 'If the true is what is grounded, then the ground is not yet true nor yet false'. However, he continues (*OC* 206): if someone asked, 'But is it *true* that the earth has existed for millions of years?' we might say 'yes'. His denial at *OC* 205 that the ground can be said to be true or false is the denial that such matters are the subjects of investigation or confirmation. This is, again, part of his fundamental point that the system does not rest on what we can know to be true, but on what we do. (Compare *OC* 411, the end of *OC* 279 and *OC* 143.)

If someone did doubt that the earth had been in existence some short time ago, then he would not only be bringing into question all the facts of history, geology, and much else besides, but would be doubting the *whole system* of evidence and verification in these areas (cf. *OC* 231, 185, 188). Such a person could have a doubt which arose from a system of belief in which our methods of evidence did not count in the same way (as did a fundamentalist like Philip Gosse, who claimed to believe that the world was created in 4004 BC), or he could have a philosophical doubt, as Russell did, who claimed that it is logically possible to doubt that the earth was in existence six minutes ago on the grounds that it could have come into existence five minutes ago, complete with all fossils, memories and records. Russell's claim to be able to doubt such a thing was discussed in Units 11–13, page 62: there is a discussion there of Wittgenstein's view, reported by Moore, that Russell was rendering meaningless the statement 'The world began more than five minutes ago' by refusing to admit as evidence for it what we all admit as evidence. Wittgenstein's reply to Russell in *On Certainty* would be somewhat different. He would no longer hold that whether a proposition was meaningful or not depended on whether there was evidence for or against it. The belief that the earth existed long before Moore's birth isn't supported by evidence (it doesn't have grounds: cf. *OC* 91) in the way the particular facts of geology or history are supported. Rather, we can cite the chronological details concerning events in the distant and recent past, as evidence for the facts of history, only if a proposition such as that the earth has existed for a long time is *not* brought into question.

As I have repeated throughout these units, the sceptic (on this occasion, Russell) is seeking to cut out dependence on evidence altogether, on the grounds that it is unreliable in principle. As Stuart Brown puts it in Units 11–13, Russell is contemplating a vantage-point from which the evidence counts for nothing, so that the 'reality' with which any proposition is supposed to agree, if it is to be seen at all, is to be seen from this vantage-point. But, to return to *OC* 191, to ask whether the proposition that the earth has existed since a long time before Moore's birth 'agrees with reality' (or with the facts) is to move around the circle of asking whether it agrees with the facts as they are established in terms of the system in which this proposition plays a fundamental role.

Against all these remarks, however, which support the idea that you cannot speak of the validity of correctness of a whole system of evidence or verification, Wittgenstein says at *OC* 286 that if we compare 'our system of knowledge' with that of people who believe it is possible to get to the moon,

then 'theirs is evidently the poorer one by far'. The suggestion is that their
system of knowledge is poorer in so far as 'there is much that they don't
know'. Wittgenstein does allow here, then, that certain beliefs fundamental
to a system of knowledge are wrong, in so far as they can be seen to arise
from ignorance (though, of course, it's ironical that it was Wittgenstein
himself who was ignorant about the possibility of travel to the moon).
However, at *OC* 238 Wittgenstein says that if someone claimed that he had
at some time been on the moon, or that the earth came into existence with
his birth, then 'he might be contradicting my fundamental attitudes. And if
he were, I should have to put up with it.' And at *OC* 239 he says that the
doctrine of transubstantiation is contradicted by someone who does not share
the Catholic system of belief and way of life. From these remarks it is obvious
that he recognizes that different systems of belief come into conflict, but his
view, leaving aside the point about the poverty of a system at *OC* 286, is that
there is no systematic means of resolving such conflicts. To undermine a
person's system of beliefs is, rather, a matter of *persuasion* (*OC* 262 and *OC*
612) or conversion—that is, a matter of getting him to see connections[1]
where he didn't see them before and getting him to recognize as evidence
what he would not previously have recognized, this being done by means
which fall short of proof or the giving of reasons why he *must* see things that
way.

It is this view that there are alternative but incompatible systems of
knowledge and belief, and no objective means of deciding between them,
which has exposed Wittgenstein to the charge of relativism.

5.4   RELATIVISM

The accusation of relativism has most commonly been levelled against
Wittgensteinian thinking in cases where Wittgenstein's ideas about meaning
and knowledge have been applied to questions in the areas of religious belief,
the philosophy of the social sciences and, especially, the methodology of
anthropology and ethics. In the bibliography I have listed some of the
relevant books. The application of Wittgenstein's ideas to the understanding
of society and to the beliefs and customs of other cultures has been worked
out by Peter Winch. What Winch has said has been criticized, particularly
on the grounds that his views are open to the charge of relativism, by Ernest
Gellner, Alan Ryan and Roger Trigg, among others. The book edited by
Bryan Wilson, listed in the bibliography, contains some of the writings of
Peter Winch along with several critical articles.

The term 'relativism' has been used in many contexts in the history of ideas.
For example, the classical philosopher Protagoras is reputed to have held the
view that the truth of any judgement is relative to the point of view of the
person making it. It is clear, from Wittgenstein's repeated insistence, in his
later works, that for it to be possible to make any judgement at all there has
to be a community of people sharing a common way of life, that he is
himself opposed to this Protagorean form of relativism or subjectivism,
according to which meaning and truth are relative to the *individual's* isolated
experiences. However, since he says that a judgement has to be made in
terms of a system of evidence shared by a community of people, and that
different groups of people—or different societies—can have different systems
and forms of life, it has seemed to some that he is committed to the view that
the truth of a judgement is relative to the beliefs and practices of a particular
society. If this interpretation is right, then Wittgenstein is committed to the

[1] See, again, the appendix by Stuart Brown.

view that, when we meet people from different cultures who seem to hold beliefs which are radically at odds with our own, we can only say that these beliefs are false in terms of our own system of judgement: in terms of *their* system, the beliefs are true. The propositions in question, which they believe and we don't, seem to be both true and false. This is patently an absurd position. Wittgenstein himself once mentions relativity in parenthesis to a remark at *Zettel* 432, which is quoted in Units 16–19 on page 44, and discussed in section 2.5 of those units.

I said in section 5.2 that Wittgenstein denies that there is any sense to the question, 'But is there no objective truth?', if behind this question is the implication that there must be some way of stepping outside all systems of judgement in order to establish which is the correct one. And I claimed that, in making this denial, Wittgenstein was specifically arguing against those philosophical views of meaning and truth which attempt to found all knowledge and belief, in a holistic way, on a set of logically indubitable propositions whose sense is not dependent on their place in any system of knowledge. For Wittgenstein, a belief or judgement is objectively certain if it has been conclusively established as true by means of the appropriate, and commonly accepted, methods—for example, by the methods of science. Something is merely subjectively certain if someone has simply satisfied himself that it is true: he may, after all, have overlooked something which someone else may point out to him. James Bogen, in a review of *On Certainty* in the *Philosophical Review* in 1966, concludes that the book leaves open the question; 'Can a sceptic use the possibility of a development or change in our conceptual scheme to show that our beliefs are not ideally warranted?' Wittgenstein does not leave this question open, however; on the contrary he explicitly deals with it at *OC* 599, 605 and 606. At *OC* 599 he says that the fact that we can cite many examples of things which people have held to be certain, but which have later proved false, is no argument for the claim that what is objectively certain is certain only on the basis of what *we* hold to be grounds. Such examples provide no basis for assuming that I may be wrong about my most fundamental beliefs (*OC* 600). On Wittgenstein's account, the ultimate court of appeal in deciding for or against the truth of my proposition is the actual way in which people go about establishing it. But for someone to say from this (*OC* 599) that 'in the end we can only adduce such grounds as *we* hold to be grounds' is not in fact to make any significant contrast with any other possibility—*unless* with the view that the way in which we speak is justified by being anchored in some metaphysical or transcendental account of 'reality' such as Wittgenstein rejects. Throughout *On Certainty* Wittgenstein is at pains to show that a language-game, or the way we speak in a particular situation about what is true, cannot, and need not, have any such justification. To think that it does is the misunderstanding referred to at *OC* 599.

One recent book which makes the case against relativism particularly clearly and convincingly is Roger Trigg's *Reason and Commitment*.[1] He writes:

> One popular form of relativism apparently manages to avoid [the] slide into total subjectivism [by] making reasoning as well as truth relative to groups or societies. Proponents of this position are usually very reluctant to be called relativists. Nevertheless, once it is stressed that different cultures have different concepts, and that their members see the world differently, it is no very great step to saying that there is no *right* way of seeing the world and that it is pure arrogance to assume that one's own society's understanding of things is the

[1] Cambridge, 1973.

correct one. It thus becomes impossible to judge other cultures at all, since to do so we would have to rely on our own conception of what is really the case, and this is to beg the question as to who is right. What we are left with are separate ways of thinking about the world, or a particular part of it. There can be no neutral way of describing the world, against which every conceptual scheme can be measured. It is obvious that we can only describe the world by means of some conceptual scheme, and so it is logically impossible to step outside every conceptual system... The result is that we are apparently left imprisoned within our own system, unable to pass judgement on other systems without using our own. This is fine if ours enables us to think of reality as it is, while other systems give a false picture. Since, however, the adherents to each system are liable to think that theirs sets the standard of truth, an obvious compromise is to say that there is no such thing as truth when conceptual systems are being compared. Each system sets its own standard of truth, but is not itself the kind of thing which can be true or false. Such a position seems to be a paradigm case of relativism. (page 6)

Trigg later offers a more detailed argument for the view that 'different concepts mean different worlds':

If the members of different societies live in 'different worlds' and do not merely have varying and conflicting beliefs about the same reality, there will not necessarily be any point of contact between the concepts of one society and those of another. If different societies are dealing with the same world, it is possible in principle to examine how differently they describe the same things. All that is necessary is to see what members of the respective societies say when confronted with a specified situation, such as a cat on a mat. The words of one group can then be regarded as a translation of the words of the other. If the assumption concerning the objectivity of what they describe is removed, there can be no justification for comparing what they say, because they may be talking about totally different things. In these circumstances, instead of their concepts depending on the composition of the world, the concepts determine the composition. Different concepts, therefore, mean a different world, so that what the world is like is relative to a conceptual system and the language of the system. (page 14f.)

Do you think that this account characterizes Wittgenstein's views in *On Certainty?*

Later in his book, Trigg takes Wittgenstein and certain 'Wittgensteinian' philosophers as examples of those who have adopted such a position. It is not at all clear, however, that he is right in doing so. For although it is certainly true that Wittgenstein stresses that different cultures can have different concepts and that there is no neutral way of comparing them, he is not obviously saying, or implying, that the people in such cultures see the world differently in any sense that commits him to relativism.

Trigg uses the notions of 'reality' and 'the world' in a quite general and comprehensive way; that is, he doesn't speak about different aspects of reality or the different sorts of things and situations that are to be found in the world. A group of people, for example, is one of the many items which make up 'the world', alongside such things as cats on mats. With this group of people, though, one can attend to their height and weight, to their nationality, or to their feelings and intentions. In each case one can distinguish between a true and a false description and between the real and unreal. Now, although in one sense such descriptions and distinctions would be of the same situation, namely a group of people, the concepts used in each description, and the criteria for distinguishing between the real and the unreal, would be different. For instance, we can say that that is not a real person, because it's a waxwork; or we can say that he is not a real person, because he continually dissembles his feelings to himself. (We can, however, say the first thing as a metaphorical way of saying the second, so linking the two senses of 'unreal'.) The fact that there are different criteria for the real and the unreal, depending on the different sorts of things being contrasted, might be expressed by saying that there are different realities here, or different aspects of the same reality.

Trigg might agree that this sense of 'different realities' is unobjectionable and doesn't give rise to the sorts of problem about conflicting beliefs which interest him. When Wittgenstein speaks of different language-games and different systems of belief (such as the system of concepts used to describe what people feel, or the different one used to describe people's physical characteristics), the language-games and systems involve concepts with a different grammar, but they are not *rivals* in the sense which interests Trigg either. At *OC* 93–95 and at other places, however, Wittgenstein does speak in a general way of a *Weltbild* (or picture of the world), but he is not, I think, using this notion in the simplistic sense in which I think Trigg uses it. For this picture is formed in terms of a huge complex of different but overlapping systems of belief—overlapping in the sense that a system of belief and enquiry about what a person *feels* is different from, but closely related to, the system of truths about his *physiology* or *physical appearance*. In these three overlapping systems we use *different concepts*; they are different in the sense that they are not subject to the same rules of grammar, but talk of different concepts in this sense is not tantamount to talking about 'different worlds'. The 'conceptual systems' here can interweave with each other in any actual discourse concerning people. They do have their own standards of truth, but only in the sense that how one measures someone's height is irrelevant to determining how he feels. They are only seen as competing systems if one attempts to reduce all modes of explanation and enquiry to one sort, that is, if one attempts to account for 'reality' as that which is comprehensively described by, for example, the language of the physical sciences.

Trigg wants to concentrate on those cases in which, it is supposed, different concepts are used to speak of the *same thing*, where 'the same thing' doesn't mean different aspects of the same thing but the very same aspect. He speaks of the assumption of objectivity' in relation to what is described and says that if this assumption is removed then there can be no justification for comparing what two groups of people, using two different sets of concepts, say. In a way, he is right; if the concepts are radically different, then there is no reason to say that the two groups are talking about the same things. For the principle of identity for any object is given in terms of the grammatical rules for the use of the relevant concept. However, this does not take Trigg's argument through. The main distortion, I think, of the case as he presents it is that *he speaks of the problem as one of translation*. If we think of two different sets of concepts, say the psychological and the physical, i.e. two language-games, then no question of translation, of one set into the other, arises. However, presenting the case in terms, not of two language-games, but of two languages, in the sense that English and Greek are two languages, leads to the erroneous assumption that there can always be—as in many cases there is—an equivalent language-game or system of enquiry in each community. But we cannot, for instance, translate the concepts used in quantum physics into an aboriginal language; there is no place for them. *A fortiori*, no question of the truth or falsity of claims made in quantum physics can arise in the aboriginal language, and so, in particular, it makes no sense to say that the claims of quantum physics are 'false for them'. A particular society may use concepts as part of a system of belief which is interwoven with a quite distinctive kind of social organization and involvement with the environment, one with no counterpart in another society, and the more remote the culture, the more this is possible. We should not expect translation between all parts of the two languages of two societies which are remote from one another in this way and which engage in quite different activities. But this fact does not lead to the supposition that these two peoples, in anything but a poetic sense, live in 'different worlds'. Rather, 'the world' is such that it contains a diversity of ways of conducting a life and relating to it.

Trigg continues by citing Peter Winch as an example of one who 'treads the relativist path', insofar as Winch

> refuses to separate 'reality' from language, so that language actually seems to determine what is real. Even an objectivist, of course, would admit that there is a close link between a language and what is regarded as real. A language expresses a community's beliefs about reality. The objectivist, however, would still wish to insist that 'reality' existed apart from people's beliefs, and that their beliefs could be mistaken. An essential function of language, he would maintain, is to concern itself with what actually is the case. Its business is to attempt to communicate *truth*. Winch will have none of this. He says 'reality is not what gives language sense. What is real and what is unreal shows itself *in* the sense that language has. Further, both the distinction between the real and the unreal and the concept of agreement with reality themselves belong to our language'[1]. It follows that different languages cannot be thought of as different attempts to describe the same reality. 'Reality' is made relative to a language and if different languages portray 'the world' differently, then there must be different worlds. If one accepts this conclusion, one is remorselessly driven to unpalatable consequences. The result of granting that 'the world' or 'reality' cannot be conceived as independent of all conceptual schemes is that there is no reason to suppose that what the peoples of very different communities see as the world is similar in any way. (page 15)

Trigg later agrees (page 16) that the 'objectivist' he speaks of must accept that it is impossible to argue outside all conceptual frameworks in order to decide between them, and, in the passage above, he agrees that there is a close link between a language and what is regarded as real. But he describes his view by saying that *languages express a community's belief about reality* and that *different languages are different attempts to describe the same reality*. It is no part of Peter Winch's view that *language* expresses beliefs about reality; language does not describe reality—rather, the speaker of a language can express his beliefs or describe something in that language, and the belief but not the language can be true or false.

At *OC* 595, however, Wittgenstein does speak of being able to say that the way a person thinks and speaks can be regarded as being in contradiction to the world that surrounds him. This indicates that he does recognize cases in which a person's 'view of reality' can be said to be radically, or even systematically, distorted. The case at *OC* 595, however, is not a case in which the person's *concepts* are at odds with 'reality', but one in which what he says or thinks, *using the same concepts as other people*, does not accord with how things are. I conjecture that cases in which one person's thoughts and sayings are isolated from those of others in this comprehensive way are cases in which we invoke the notion of insanity. In such cases there is no easy method of

---

[1] Winch, 'Understanding a Primitive Society', in *Rationality*, ed. B. Wilson, Blackwell, page 82.

correcting what the person says, though it may be possible to trace a complex of attitudes and feelings which can be seen as underpinning the distortion in beliefs.

What I have said, however, may seem to avoid Trigg's question whether or not the beliefs which go with an activity or practice are false. At *OC* 609 Wittgenstein cites the case of a people which is not guided in its actions by the propositions of physics but consults oracles. He goes on to say that if we call this practice wrong (as Trigg wants to do in the example above) then we are just using our own language-game as a basis from which to *combat* theirs. And at *OC* 611 he says that when two principles meet which cannot be reconciled, then each man calls the other names, just as Trigg does in the next passage I quote. At *OC* 612 Wittgenstein contrasts 'combating' the other with giving him *reasons*: you cannot give the other man reasons why he *must* see the facts in one connection rather than another. In particular, you cannot accuse him of holding beliefs which 'do not correspond with reality'.

There is a more extensive collection of Wittgenstein's notes on this issue of understanding radically different forms of practice, which he made in connection with his reading of Sir James Frazer's *The Golden Bough*.[1] One of his main ideas in these notes is that Frazer's account of the magical and religious notions of man is unsatisfactory because it makes them appear as *mistakes* and views them as though they were false hypotheses about 'the physics of things'. Again the issue of *translation* is relevant. Their beliefs can only be translated into ours, and assessed, if there are activities and practices in our society which play the same role for us as they do for them. A belief may not always function, for example, as a scientific hypothesis. Someone who believes that the earth is flat, to use Trigg's example (page 18), can be shown to be wrong, quite straightforwardly on Wittgenstein's account, if his belief can, without distortion, be seen as part of a *hypothesis* on the *basis of known fact*. Trigg presents this case in a way which cannot be so construed: the 'committed flat-earther' is a person who has access to the same evidence that we have. Trigg writes:

> There are two possibilities left in the face of such an apparently insoluble disagreement. The first is to accept the relativist position that there is more than one way of ultimately looking at the matter. One may be a committed flat-earther or a committed round-earther and our view of what is to count as evidence stems from these commitments. The second course is to accept that the round-earther has made his case, and that the flat-earther is just *wrong*. The mere fact that what the round-earther said was not acceptable to the flat-earther does not in any way suggest that he is assuming the truth of what he is trying to prove. It could merely show that the flat-earther is so pig-headed that he cannot recognize truth when it is presented to him.

This has a solid ring of common sense about it. It seems perverse to withhold saying that the flat-earther is just wrong. But where did he go wrong? At what point did he make a mistake? One thing which makes it easy to say that he is just wrong is that we suspect that, at some level, his belief is based on a prejudice the causes of which he doesn't recognize. We think that someone qualified to do so would be able to *explain* why he holds so persistently to this system of beliefs which is so much at odds with the beliefs of the community in which he is living. In many cases, the reasons why someone holds an eccentric belief can be fitted in with other things we know. I myself would extend the range of such cases wider than Wittgenstein possibly would. For instance, on the face of it at least, I find the idea

[1] The notes are published in German in the journal *Synthese*, vol. xvii, 1967.

convincing that mediaeval European belief in witchcraft can be explained by some description of the social relationships between people and by the phenomenon of psychological projection of fears and anxieties. But I have to concede two points about this. First, such beliefs were possible—the concepts made sense—only in the wider context of mediaeval religious belief. Second, in using a concept like 'projection' I have described the situation in terms of my own system of understanding of human motivation.

Of the sorts of cases discussed by Frazer,[1] Wittgenstein says that it is misleading to see the beliefs and rituals as mistakes or hypotheses. By contrast, Wittgenstein says that where a ritualistic practice goes together with a belief about incarnation, well-being or whatever, the practice is not *based on the belief*, but 'both of them are there'. Frazer's picture is of a people which engages in activities informed by beliefs which, according to the standards of science, are palpably false; he isolates the beliefs in order to *explain* the practice. We are not helped by Frazer's explanation, says Wittgenstein, because we are referred from an incomprehensible activity to an apparently absurd belief. For example, Frazer speaks of certain activities being dictated by fear of the ghost of the slain, thus using the notion of a *ghost* as an explanation. But if this is to be an explanation, one has to understand the concepts used in it in some context other than merely that of the practice being explained. Further, says Wittgenstein, an explanation can only explain if it finally appeals to 'an inclination in ourselves'. Thus Frazer's use of the notion of a ghost in his explanation shows that he too shares an understanding of the primitive responses to the world that can be given expression by the use of such notions. (This is not to say that Frazer must have believed in ghosts.) The rituals or practices, then, are not *based on* beliefs such as the belief that there are such things as ghosts, so that, if this belief can be shown to be false, then the practices can be shown to be without foundation; rather, both the belief and the practice are the natural expression of responses which are neither true nor false.

Wittgenstein, in other words, talks of these different and alien practices, not as different ways of describing or presenting a theory about 'reality', but as different developments of attitudes, responses and feelings which we all share regarding characteristic human situations and predicaments in the world. In the case of the example of consulting oracles (*OC* 609), Wittgenstein is not saying anything so obscure (as Trigg would have him say) as that the language used in connection with oracles is an expression of a different reality; only that beliefs about oracles do not fit into our system of physics, and that beliefs which go with any such practice can only be assessed as wrong or mistaken if they are thought of as explanatory hypotheses about nature which play the same role in the lives of the people who consult oracles as beliefs established in physics do in ours.

The views in *On Certainty*, and the way in which they are presented, are a further articulation of Wittgenstein's commitment to the idea that, in the end, both the person trying to understand another culture *and the philosopher*—who is like a stranger in his own language—can only *describe* and say: human life is like that. It is this which is at the focus of most criticism.

---

[1] See, for example, page 92 in Stuart Brown's appendix.

6 CONCLUSION: THE CRITICAL FOCUS

At *PI* 124 Wittgenstein says:

> Philosophy may in no way interfere with the actual use of language; it can in the end only describe it.
> For it cannot give it any foundation either.
> It leaves everything as it is.

In these units I have tried to bring out the sense in which Wittgenstein maintains that language, and in particular a language-game in which we make claims of truth or falsity, has, as he says here, no foundation. This involved him in denying the view that any valid claim to knowledge must be seen as resting ultimately on some set of ideas or propositions which are logically indubitable, in the sense in which Russell or Descartes, for instance, sought examples of logically indubitable truths in the 'basic' elements of experience, or the *cogito*, respectively. Wittgenstein's denial of this is connected with his claim that any systematic programme of philosophical scepticism, which attempts to question the validity (or diversity) of the criteria and methods used to establish the truth in any area of enquiry, proceeds only by ignoring the fact that the ways in which we speak about material objects, about what other people experience, or about what happened in the past, are not founded on certainty. The philosophical task in relation to scepticism is thus to display the connections between, and diversity of, claims to knowledge and belief in order to present a clear view of how things fit together. It would also remove the temptation to make false analogies and misleading generalizations. Many philosophers radically disagree with Wittgenstein's view of philosophical method and claim that description isn't argument. If philosophy is left at the level of describing clearly the interrelationships between things which we already know, then it can bring no change in our ideas. There is thus an accusation of conservatism. Ernest Gellner, for example, writes in direct criticism of Wittgenstein's view that one cannot seek external and general criteria for the validation of linguistic or conceptual custom, and he argues that 'philosophy must return to the place which in my view it should never have left—the attempt to formulate and defend criteria which are more than mere descriptions of *de facto* custom.'[1] This is the view I described at the beginning of the units, namely that the philosopher should see his task, in relation to the question of knowledge and certainty, as one of justifying or validating the actual criteria we use in making claims to truth. In his appendix to these units Stuart Brown discusses Wittgenstein's 'descriptive' method and suggests that such criticisms do not sufficiently take into account Wittgenstein's central notion of a *perspicuous representation*.

Many philosophers also take up a critical stance towards Wittgenstein's view of meaning, and seek to replace it with one in which the notion of truth is central. Such philosophers are working on the programme of developing a general theory of truth for any language. It is against the background of such work that Sam Guttenplan, in the next and final unit, examines in detail the role which the notion of truth plays in Wittgenstein's writings.

---

[1] The New Idealism, op. cit., page 139.

APPENDIX

PHILOSOPHY AS 'THE NATURAL HISTORY OF HUMAN BEINGS'
by Stuart Brown

Wittgenstein's critics accuse him of abandoning the true function of philosophy for a 'merely descriptive' method. Wittgenstein, they say, is content to describe, whereas the true task of philosophy is to justify and to explain. A major theme of Wittgenstein's *On Certainty* is that there are limits to what can be doubted and that therefore there has to be an end at some point to justification. Philosophy, according to Wittgenstein, does not provide a foundation for science. Neither should it model itself upon the methods of science. It is in connection with this latter point that Wittgenstein insists that the job of philosophy is 'descriptive' rather than explanatory, as in the following passage:

> Our craving for generality has another main source: our preoccupation with the method of science. I mean the method of reducing the explanation of natural phenomena to the smallest possible number of primitive natural laws; and, in mathematics, of unifying the treatment of different topics by using a generalization. Philosophers constantly see the method of science before their eyes, and they are irresistibly tempted to ask and answer questions in the way science does. This tendency is the real source of metaphysics, and leads the philosopher into complete darkness. I want to say here that it can never be our job to reduce anything to anything, or to explain anything. Philosophy really *is* 'purely descriptive'. *(BB* 18)

In these remarks Wittgenstein appears to deny to the philosopher any interesting or difficult role. This is because, in denying that it is the job of the philosopher to explain anything, Wittgenstein makes it look as if the philosopher is not attempting to reach a better understanding. His stress on philosophy being 'purely descriptive' is often taken as encouragement to taking things at their face value. Wittgenstein suggested at one point that what he was supplying was really 'remarks on the natural history of human beings' (*PI* 415). Philosophy thus has an affinity with anthropology. Only the philosopher does not contribute 'curiosities'. All he contributes are 'observations which no one has doubted, which have escaped remark only because they are always before our eyes'. (*PI* 415) This remark encourages the impression that Wittgenstein thought that the philosopher was like a social anthropologist, except that the philosopher only tells us what we know already.

These impressions of what Wittgenstein is saying lead to the charge that his account makes philosophy trivial, because it is 'purely descriptive' of what we already know; uncritically conservative, because philosophy 'leaves everything as it is' (*PI* 124); and relativistic, because on such an account the description of what people are doing has to be couched in terms which belong to one of their language-games. An explanatory theory promises a point of view from which it would be possible to criticize such descriptions and indeed replace them by more accurate ones. In ruling out such an explanatory role in philosophy and, perhaps, in social anthropology too, Wittgenstein seems to be making the standards of 'accurate description' relative to language-games.

Such charges, though commonly made, are not entirely clear. And indeed I think they betray a misunderstanding of what Wittgenstein means by 'description' and what he means by his insistence that we must '*do away with all explanation*' in philosophy. (*PI* 109) I think that, on a proper understanding, Wittgenstein is not exposed to these charges. Although he himself said, in his 1932–33 lectures, that what he was offering was a 'synopsis of trivialities', he made it clear at the same time that it was very difficult to do this.[1] As we shall see, the kind of 'synopsis' which Wittgenstein thought philosophy should provide was one which furthers our understanding by enabling us to see connections which we did not formerly see. The first criticism is one which evaporates once it is made clearer what kind of understanding Wittgenstein thought philosophy could provide. The other two criticisms are interconnected. Critics of Wittgenstein have written as though he must have believed that rituals and ritual beliefs are in some way 'self-validating' and as if we could only understand those of primitive peoples by entering into their 'form of life'. I think that, while Wittgenstein did indeed believe that many rituals and ritual beliefs do not require justification, it is not because he thought they were in any sense 'self-validating'. Rather, since he did not think that such ritual beliefs were a kind of 'opinion', he did not conceive of rituals or ritual beliefs as either admitting of criticism or validation. Nor did he hold that understanding the behaviour of alien peoples was a matter of effecting an esoteric entry into their 'form of life'. Our understanding of such people is, on the contrary, based on our common humanity.

When Wittgenstein speaks of doing away with all 'explanation' and of not advancing any kind of 'theory', as he does in *PI* 109, he is turning his back on the kind of reductive explanation which is offered in physics. From the context of *PI* 109, it is clear that Wittgenstein regarded the *Tractatus* as being theoretical and explanatory in a reductive way. For the *Tractatus* sought to show that underlying the manifest diversity of forms of langage there was an essential unity. This unity was given by the general form of propositions. The *Tractatus* both explained the nature of propositions and provided a theory which showed what all propositions had in common, which could therefore show the limits of what could be said. When Wittgenstein says: 'Philosophy simply puts everything before us, and neither explains nor deduces anything' (*PI* 126), he is intimating a project which is quite different from that of the *Tractatus*. Indeed, the purpose of the 'descriptions' which the philosopher gives is to correct the kind of misunderstanding which is embodied in the belief that one has got to the essence of something in philosophy. Wittgenstein makes it clear, in *PI* 109, that a 'description' gets its light from 'philosophical problems'. A description, moreover, only serves this purpose if the facts are *arranged* in a particular way. Philosophy would indeed be a boring subject if it was concerned *only* with telling people what they knew already. The difficulty, and the interest, of philosophy, as Wittgenstein saw it, lies in trying to get the right *arrangement* of what we have always known.

It is by 'arranging what we have always known' that we are enabled to '*command a clear view* of the use of our words'. (*PI* 122) It is for this reason that Wittgenstein holds that the concept of 'perspicuous representation'[2] is of fundamental importance. This is a notion which is discussed earlier in the course (Units 14–15, section 3.4) in relation to 'proposition' and 'number'. But there are many places in Wittgenstein's later writings where he attempts

---

[1] See G. E. Moore's notes, 'Wittgenstein's Lectures in 1930–33' in *Philosophical Papers*, by G. E. Moore, Allen & Unwin, 1959, page 323.

[2] Wittgenstein's translators sometimes give 'synoptic' for 'perspicuous' (see *Z* 273, *Z* 464) in related contexts. Wittgenstein's own preference seems to have been for the word 'synopsis' but this has misleading connotations.

to produce such an arrangement. We need the kind of understanding of what a proposition is which enables us to see how grammatical propositions and empirical propositions are both kinds of proposition. A 'perspicuous representation' brings out the family resemblances between different kinds of proposition. Other concepts which seem to be treated by Wittgenstein in a similar way are those of 'expectation' and 'meaning' in the *Blue Book* as well as such concepts as those of 'understanding' and 'reading' in the *Philosophical Investigations*. (See respectively *PI* 38 to 155, and *PI* 156 to 178.)

It is, I think, significant that Wittgenstein stresses the importance of 'perspicuous representation' not only in a passage in which he is engaging in the philosophy of philosophy but also in a very different context, in his 'Remarks on Frazer's *Golden Bough*'. *The Golden Bough* (1922) is a work of historical anthropology. Here is the relevant passage from these 'Remarks':[1]

> The concept of a perspicuous representation is of fundamental significance for us. It earmarks the form of account we give, the way we look at things. (A kind of 'Weltanschauung' that seems to be typical of our time. Spengler.)

> A perspicuous representation produces just that understanding which consists in 'seeing connections'. Hence the importance of finding and inventing *intermediate cases*.

PI 122 begins with two sentences that are not included in the passage I have just quoted. As these sentences do relate particularly to the philosophy of philosophy their absence in the other context is not surprising. Otherwise the most conspicuous difference is one of order. The first three sentences of the passage just quoted correspond to the last three sentences of *PI* 122. The second paragraph of the passage just quoted corresponds to the third and fourth sentences of *PI* 122.

Of these five corresponding sentences three are exactly the same. The differences affect the final sentences of each paragraph. Only in the *Investigations* passage is there a reference to *inventing* 'intermediate cases' as well as finding them. In the passage from these Remarks on Frazer's *'Golden Bough'*, in the second place, Wittgenstein does not simply *ask* whether the way we look at things is a 'Weltanschauung' but says that it *is* a kind of 'Weltanschauung' that seems to be typical of our time. He also adds the name 'Spengler', a reference to the philosopher/historian Oswald Spengler (1880–1936), author of *The Decline of the West*.

A comparison of these passages does, I believe, throw some light on how Wittgenstein saw the affinity between philosophy and anthropology and how far we may take his suggestion that what he is doing is supplying 'remarks on the natural history of human beings'. (*PI* 415) It seems from these passages that Wittgenstein thought of philosophy and anthropology as properly directed towards producing a similar kind of understanding, namely, one which enables us to see connections between the data before us. The difference between the two which marks out philosophy as a non-empirical discipline lies in the licence which the philosopher has to invent 'intermediate cases'. This is, I think, why Wittgenstein says, at a later point, that 'We are not doing natural science; nor yet natural history—since we can also invent fictitious natural history for our own purposes.' (*PI* page 230) This shows how misleading Wittgenstein's use of the word 'descriptive' to characterize his own method is. For what we call a description is commonly

---

[1] The German text was published in *Synthese*, Vol. 17 (1967), pp. 233–53. There is a translation, by Rush Rhees and A. C. Miles, in *The Human World* No. 3 for May 1971. I will elsewhere quote from this translation, but in this passage I have followed the idiom of the translator of the *Philosophical Investigations*.

something which meets certain scholarly standards of factual accuracy. But Wittgenstein evidently intends that there could be descriptions of purely imaginary examples. He is indeed quite explicit about this at the end of the first part of *The Brown Book*, where he is talking about the account he has given of words such as 'deriving' and 'reading'. Such an account, he writes,

> essentially consists in describing a selection of examples exhibiting characteristic features, some examples showing these features in exaggeration, others showing transitions, certain series of examples showing the trailing off of such features. Imagine someone wished to give you an idea of the facial characteristics of a certain family, the So and so's, he would do it by showing you a set of family portraits and by drawing your attention to certain characteristic features, and his main task would consist in the proper *arrangement* of these pictures, which e.g., will enable you to see how certain influences gradually changed the features, in what characteristic ways the members of the family aged, what features appeared more strongly as they did so. (*BB* 125)

The purpose of such an 'arrangement' is to enable us to see the connections between the different cases. One might think, for example, that the case where a person knows something by heart and says what is on the page before him is not a case of reading but that reading proper involves no guessing from the context, knowing by heart, or whatever. This is the kind of place where Wittgenstein considers it appropriate to describe 'intermediary cases' (BB 122). Some of Wittgenstein's own cases, however, are purely imaginary. (For example, the case where animals are used as 'reading machines' in *BB* 120.)

Wittgenstein seems to have thought that the proper task of anthropology, like philosophy, was to describe rather than to explain. Indeed, he suggests, as one reason why the attempt to find an explanation is wrong, that 'we have only to put together in the right way what we *know* without adding anything, and the satisfaction we are trying to get from the explanation comes of itself'. ('Remarks', *op. cit.* page 30) Frazer's project, by contrast, was precisely to *explain* why it was that the practices of the priesthood of Nemi existed. Here is how Frazer described his enterprise:

> ... recent researches into the early history of man have revealed an essential similarity with which, under many superficial differences, the human mind has elaborated its first crude philosophy of life. Accordingly, if we can show that a barbarous custom, like that of the priesthood of Nemi, has existed elsewhere; if we can prove that these motives have operated widely, perhaps universally, in human society, producing in varied circumstances a variety of institutions specifically different but generally alike; if we can show, lastly, that these very motives, with some of their derivative institutions, were actually at work in classical antiquity; then we may fairly infer that at a remoter age the same motives gave birth to the priesthood of Nemi. (*The Golden Bough*, Macmillan paperback edition, page 2f.)

These statements do, it seems to me, bring out the kind of understanding which Frazer thought appropriate. He was looking for a theoretical and historical explanation in terms of the 'primitive mind of man' and his 'first crude philosophy of life'. He was attempting to do in anthropology what Wittgenstein came to think he himself had erroneously sought to do in the *Tractatus*, namely, produce a reductive account. Notice the contrast in the above quotation between 'essential similarity' and 'superficial differences'. Wittgenstein does not deny that Frazer was offering *an* arrangement of the data he had collected. Frazer's mistake was to think he had found, in his account of the 'primitive mind of man', *the* explanation for the kinds of practice he had been studying. But his kind of account, according to Wittgenstein, was not the only one. 'An historical explanation, an explanation as a hypothesis of the development, is only *one* kind of summary of the data—of their synopsis.' (op. cit., page 34) I think his view was that it is 'typical of our time' (i.e. of what Spengler refers to as 'Faustian [Western] man') to want *this* kind of summary of the data. If so, Wittgenstein evidently regarded himself as at odds with the 'Weltanschauung' he alludes to. For it is clear that, to his mind, Frazer's account did not enhance our understanding but, on the contrary, obscured it. Frazer's imagination was captivated by a 'picture' of the essence of magic which prevented him from having a 'clear view' of the data he had collected. He sought an 'explanation' where what was needed was a 'perspicuous representation'. We do not need, and should not look for such an explanation. We can do what needs to be done

> just by arranging the factual material so that we can easily pass from one part to another and have a clear view of it—showing it in a 'perspicuous' way. ('Remarks'. *op. cit.*, page 35)

Frazer, throughout *The Golden Bough*, characteristically seeks to explain a ritual practice by reference to some opinion or superstition which informs it. For example, he writes:

> A savage hardly conceives the distinction commonly drawn by more advanced peoples between the natural and the supernatural. To him the world is to a great extent worked by supernatural agents, that is, by personal beings acting on impulses and motives like his own, liable like him to be moved by appeals to their pity, their hopes, and their fears. In a world so conceived he sees no limit to his power of influencing the course of nature to his own advantage. Prayers, promises, or threats may secure him fine weather and an abundant crop from the gods; and if a god should happen, as he sometimes believes, to become incarnate in his own person, then he need appeal to no higher being; he, the savage, possesses in himself all the powers necessary to further his own well-being and that of his fellow-man. (Paperback edition, page 13)

It is with this sort of claim, on Frazer's part, in mind that Wittgenstein writes:

> ...one might begin a book on anthropology in this way: When we watch the life and behaviour of men all over the earth we see that apart from what we might call animal activities, taking food etc., etc., men also carry out actions that bear a peculiar character and might be called ritualistic.

> But then it is nonsense if we go on to say that the characteristic feature of *these* actions is that they spring from wrong ideas about the physics of things. (This is what Frazer does when he says magic is really false physics, or as the case may be, false medicine, technology, etc.)

> What makes the character of ritual action is not any view or opinion, either right or wrong, although an opinion—a belief—itself can be ritualistic, or belong to a rite. ('Remarks', *op. cit.*, page 33)

Wittgenstein wanted to say that an understanding of ritual action involved seeing how it belonged to a family of such actions some of which we find amongst ourselves. Understanding a ritual practice, therefore, involves 'seeing the connection' between it and practices of our own. We can, according to Wittgenstein, even imagine primitive practices ourselves and 'it would only be by chance if they were not actually to be found somewhere'. (*op. cit.*, page 32) Wittgenstein goes on:

That is, the principle according to which these practices are ordered is much more general than Frazer shows it to be. And we find it in ourselves: we can think out for ourselves the different possibilities.—We can readily imagine that, say, in a given tribe no one is allowed to see the king, or again that every man in the tribe is obliged to see him. And then it will certainly not be left more or less to chance but the king will be *shown* to the people. Perhaps no one will be allowed to touch him or perhaps they will be *compelled* to do so. Think how after Schubert's death his brother cut certain of Schubert's notes into small pieces and gave to his favourite pupils these pieces of a few bars each. As a sign of piety this action is *just* as comprehensible to us as the other one of keeping the scores undisturbed and accessible to no one. And if Schubert's brother had burnt the scores we could still understand this as a sign of piety.

As Wittgenstein understood it, that imaginary case could serve as an 'intermediate link' between the acts of piety of Schubert's brother, which we have no difficulty in understanding, and other rituals which puzzle us. In this way a 'perspicuous representation' accomplishes what was sought for in an explanation.

Such an account does in one way understate the affinity between philosophy and anthropology. In *The Golden Bough* (page 280 ff.) Frazer gives an account of purification ceremonies which are performed on the return of a successful head hunt. These ceremonies, so Frazer tells us, are performed to appease the soul of the man whose head has been taken. 'That these observances are dictated by fear of the ghosts of the slain seems certain...'. Wittgenstein quotes this sentence and then adds:

> But why does Frazer use the word 'ghost'? He evidently understands this superstition well enough, since he uses a familiar superstitious word to describe it. Or rather, he might have seen from this that there is something in us too that speaks in support of those observances by savages. ('Remarks', *op. cit.*, page 34)

It is, I think, relevant to observe that these remarks come shortly before the 'perspicuous representation' passage. Moreover, that passage is itself immediately followed by a return to a discussion of the same practices:

> I wish to say: Nothing shows our kinship to those savages better than the fact that Frazer has at hand a word as familiar to us as 'ghost' or 'shade' to describe their views...

> What is queer in this is not limited to the expressions 'ghost' and 'shade', too little is made of the fact that we include the words 'soul' and 'spirit' in our own civilised vocabulary. Compared with this, the fact that we do not believe that our soul eats and drinks is a minor detail. (*Op. cit.*, page 35)

Wittgenstein's suggestion here seems to be that we would better understand such ceremonies as express fear of the ghosts of the slain if we understand the way in which words like 'ghost', 'shade', 'soul' and 'spirit' are used in our own language. The suggestion seems to be that we do not have a clear view of our own use of these words. Now here, as I understand him, Wittgenstein is very far from being the uncritical conservative which one might expect, to judge from his insistence that philosophy 'leaves everything as it is'. For I think it follows from his line of thinking that theories about the nature of the soul stand in the same relation to our use of the word 'soul' as the *Tractatus* theories of propositions and numbers stand to our use of the words 'proposition' and 'number'. Here too a 'picture' can hold us captive. (See *PI* 115 ff.) If we do not have a 'perspicuous representation' of our own use of the word 'soul' we shall not be able to understand the rituals of primitive peoples in relation to the souls of the departed.

Wittgenstein does not in this case provide the required arrangement of what we know already. Nor shall I attempt to do so. But here is a use of the word 'soul' which may serve as an 'intermediate case'. It is from the American Civil War song, 'John Brown's Body':

> John Brown's body lies a-mouldering in the grave,
> But his soul goes marching on.

An anthropologist from another place in the galaxy might be tempted to attribute, to the abolitionists who sang this song heartily, the belief that souls could march. We know that is quite wrong. But still we might be a little puzzled by it if we forget that it is a marching song. It is a song sung by soldiers on their way to accomplishing the work begun by John Brown. Did those soldiers *believe* that they were in some sense identical with the soul of John Brown? Perhaps we may say they did. But this is an example of a ritual belief. Neither it nor the ritual of singing the song can be said to be reasonable or unreasonable in the way in which an opinion or actions informed by opinions can be. It is a good example, to my mind, of where Wittgenstein would have said: 'We can only *describe* and say, human life is like that.' ('Remarks', *op. cit.*, page 30)

Here, in conclusion, are some of the implications I would draw from the account I have sketched of the connection, as Wittgenstein saw it, of philosophy and anthropology:

1   Wittgenstein, on my interpretation of him, offers no support to 'relativism' in social anthropology. The basis for an understanding of cultures other than our own is, according to him, our common humanity.

2   Our understanding of others should not—or at least should not paradigmatically—be modelled on the kinds of reductive explanation to be found in the physical sciences.

3   There is something like an aesthetic judgement involved in being satisfied with a perspicuous representation. At the same time there are grounds for dissatisfaction if there are puzzles which remain. For these are symptoms of the representation's not being entirely 'perspicuous'.

4   There is, in both anthropology and philosophy, an urge to accept certain 'pictures' which obscure our view of the facts we need to take account of. In each case the urge is a deep-rooted one. Language is just one of the phenomena for which a 'perspicuous representation' is needed. It is also needed for an understanding of the social practices in which language is rooted.

BIBLIOGRAPHY

Works on topics related to these units which develop some of the ideas in Wittgenstein's later philosophy

Cavell, S., 'The Avoidance of Love', in *Must We Mean What We Say?*, Scribner, 1969.
Dilman, I. *Induction and Deduction*, Blackwell, 1973.
Malcolm, N. *Knowledge and Certainty*, Prentice-Hall, 1965.
Phillips, D. Z., *The Concept of Prayer*, Routledge, 1965.
Phillips, D. Z., and Mounce, H. O., *Moral Practices*, Routledge, 1970.
Winch, P. G., *The Idea of a Social Science*, Routledge, 1958.
Winch, P. G., 'Understanding a Primitive Society', in Wilson (ed.), below.

Critical works

Gellner, E., 'The New Idealism', in *Positivism and Sociology*, A. Giddens (ed.), Heinemann, 1974.
Gellner, E., 'Concepts and Society', in Wilson (ed.), below.
Ryan, A., *Philosophy of the Social Sciences*, Macmillan, 1970.
Trigg, R., *Reason and Commitment*, Cambridge, 1973.
Wilson, B. (ed.), *Rationality*, Blackwell, 1970; contains critical and relevant articles other than those mentioned above.

A contemporary work which argues in support of scepticism

Unger, P., *Ignorance*, Oxford, 1975.

Contemporary works which take up different positions from Wittgenstein's concerning questions of meaning and truth

Evans, G., and McDowell, J. (eds.), *Truth and Meaning*, Oxford, 1975.
Guttenplan, S. (ed.), *Mind and Language*, Oxford, 1975.
Quine, W. V. O., *Word and Object*, MIT Press, 1960.
Quine, W. V. O., *Ontological Relativity and Other Essays*, Columbia University Press, 1969.
Quine, W. V. O., and Ullian, J. S., *The Web of Belief*, Random House, 1970.

THOUGHT AND REALITY: CENTRAL THEMES IN WITTGENSTEIN'S PHILOSOPHY